Lord, Shut Me Up!

Anger Management for Christians

Karen D. Wasoba

Lord, Shut Me Up!
Anger Management for Christians

Published by Wheatmark®
610 East Delano Street, Suite 104, Tucson, Arizona 85705 U.S.A.
www.wheatmark.com

ISBN: 978-1-58736-763-2
LCCN: 2006939856

The information contained within these pages was adapted from material provided by Dr. Daniel Wilkinson in his "Living Love" series. Each concept I share is a practical explanation of Dr. Dan's initial teachings on I Corinthians 13: 4–8a.

Many thanks to Dr. Gayle Wilkinson for her generous input and permission to use this material for *Lord, Shut Me Up! Anger Management for Christians.*

Contents

Lord, Shut Me Up!

This book is dedicated to my tenaciously faithful friends and family. Without you I would have had to learn this material without the benefit of your endless tolerance and unconditional love.

Acknowledgements

My gratitude begins with Harvester Christian Church, of St. Charles, Missouri. They gave me an opportunity to minister to their cherished congregation and have continued to encourage me to expand and spread my enthusiasm in liberal doses.

To the Harvester Counseling ministry for loving and protecting me through my bouts of adrenaline pumping, wild enthusiasm and utter exhaustion. Special thanks to Brian Coats who continues to simply look at me, shake his head, and laugh.

To Patti Hight, my right-hand woman (even though I'm left-handed). Her ability to make my bright ideas become reality is amazing. I'm thankful for her abilities, but especially for her sweet friendship.

To Dr. Joann McCracken, for her proofreading, editing, and generalized bullying (is there a DSM IV diagnosis for that?). Joann has been the best cheerleader a team could ever have.

To Susan Smead, for never once doubting that God could use my talents to reach and encourage people who are hurting. Thank you so much.

To Steve Knubley, my intern and coworker, for proofreading this manuscript and praising it with enthusiasm— I give you an "A."

Most importantly, I want to thank Don, Kari, and Ryan for their support of my ministry efforts over the last few years. Your encouragement as I shared my hopes and uncertainties has been deeply appreciated. Don, you're the most aggravating, dearly loved sidekick a woman could ever have! Kari and Ryan, thanks for nodding approval during my "think out loud" sessions when you had no idea what I was saying, and didn't understand the jokes that had me doubled over in hysterics. You're soooo used to me.

Thanks to you all.

ONE

Real vs. Ideal

ood Christians don't get angry. They cheerfully accept all frustrating and painful experiences in their lives as spiritual tests and pass them all without breaking a sweat. These giants of the faith quote large passages of Scripture (in several translations) on the virtues of patience and look angelic as they gaze about them benignly. They rise early to greet the day, dunking chamomile tea bags in their china cups while writing out their favorite verses in longhand. There are calluses on their knees, and their prayer lists include not only missionaries, but also their children's names, ages, and shoe sizes.

Then there are the rest of us. After falling out of bed trying to answer an insistent phone call, we stub our toes on book bags and fall over the family pet in an effort to keep the machinery of our lives humming along smoothly. We spend more time trying to salvage yesterday's hairdo than it would have taken to jump in the shower and start over. Our clothes are easily accessible, however, because they're still on the floor where we stepped out of them the night before!

We mutter under our breath when someone cuts us off in traffic, and roll our eyes in frustration when the driver in the giant dumpster on wheels in front of us decides to apply her lip liner while blocking the only exit lane. Then after we finally lose our self-control and say angry things, almost always targeting those we love most, we bury ourselves in chocolate.

We feel victimized and guilty when we review a long day of aggravation, and our less-than-stellar response to it, all the while comparing ourselves unfavorably to the "perfect Christian" we're taught we're supposed to be.

Our Bible is around here someplace—probably still in the car where we left it after church last Sunday. We don't like tea all that much, and the only time we see early morning is when we're still awake from the night before. We carry with us a sense of low-grade depression because of who we think we should be before God, all the while knowing that we are unlikely to attain that standard. No matter what our performance level is, we will never be good enough in our own estimation (and probably not in God's, either), and that hurts and annoys us even more.

We finally tire of continually promising God we'll do better, tired of turning over new leaves. We excuse our dejection by announcing that "only God is perfect." At that emotional and spiritual low point, we tend to give up in our efforts at self-control until we hear the next inspiring sermon or read the latest Christian self-help book and determine to try again to be "good Christians."

YAWWNNNN…

It gets old, doesn't it? Even as children we are raised with the expectation that whatever we attempt, we will be successful doing. As a mom, I remember vowing that my children would be the smartest, prettiest, and most accomplished individuals in the history of the world (and they *are*, but I digress...).

Of course, once they hit adolescence my husband and I were convinced we had somehow misinterpreted the instructions as we dealt with cockiness, pride, and the assumption that they were always right!

Purpose

The purpose of this book is to provide a practical resource for anyone who sincerely wants to live a genuine emotional and spiritual life, free from the bondage of uncontrolled anger. It isn't like a diet book that we clutch to our hearts with the hope that it's the final answer for all our problems and then discard when we discover we can't actually live that way; rather, it is intended to be usable and honest and provide safety as we realize that there is hope.

Men and women perceive anger differently; men interpret issues externally while women are more internal in their interpretations. For example, if a man and a woman are seated at identical computers and the machinery breaks down, the man will tend to blame the computer (or the kids, or the manual, or the manufacturer) and the woman will more likely blame herself!

I am recording these thoughts and ideas on paper to give the reader a useful and tangible guide to make it possible to control his or her behavior. It has been used successfully in my own life, my counseling practice, and in six-week classes I have taught on the subject to individuals and groups struggling in the areas of patience, anger, and self-control.

Personal Experience

I grew up in an atmosphere that was stressful and isolated. My two brothers and I were the first kids in the
neighborhood to have divorced parents, and our mother
remarried shortly after the divorce was final. Our step-dad
was withdrawn, yet when he became angry we feared for
our physical safety. My brothers were six and eight years
older than I was, so they found ways to disappear most of
the time. But I wasn't that creative and I felt the need to
be with my mom as much as I could. Mom had her own
emotional challenges, and distracted herself by drinking,
often to unconsciousness.

At that point, I would wander around our neighborhood or lose myself by reading or watching television. It
was an unspoken rule that nothing be said to others regarding the situation at home, so my relational skills with
family members or anyone else were almost nonexistent.

So it probably comes as no surprise that I was extremely immature in coping with my emotions and interactions
with others.

My nickname in third grade was "Temper Tantrum"
and I earned it every single day. Even at ten years of age
my life was in constant turmoil, not only at home but at
school too. I had no coping mechanisms, only survival
skills. There was no personal relationship with anyone,
much less God.

When the kids at school discovered my tendency to get
mad and lash out, they exploited it, teasing and pushing
me until I would lose control of myself. I reacted negatively not only to my classmates, but also to my teacher, who
tried in vain to get me to behave. Most days were spent
in the principal's office being reprimanded. Some weeks I
saw the principal more that I saw my own teacher! It got

to the point I was not allowed back in school until I visited a child psychologist, who found nothing wrong with me that a little self-control wouldn't cure.

In a new school, my fifth grade teacher instituted a punishment system of writing the name of miscreants on his desk calendar along with a word and its definition that we were to copy ten times. He jokingly said that the student with the most "punishments" at the end of the school year was his favorite. I won, by far, and was deeply insulted that there was no real prize!

You'd have thought my accepting Christ while a sophomore in high school would resolve my sense of aggravation and anger, but it didn't. It only added guilt to the equation as I then realized that when I opened my mouth I wasn't only displeasing myself, my friends, and my family, but now God as well.

Even with this sense of failure underlying every accomplishment, I managed to attend, and graduate from, a fundamental Bible college and marry a man devoted to me and our family.

My husband, Don, didn't like my frequent flare-ups and nastiness when I lost my temper, but managed to survive even when I was at my verbal worst.

It wasn't until we had been married for almost fourteen years, and had two children, that I was introduced to a sincere Christian counselor, Dr. Dan Wilkinson. He introduced me to the concept of patience and stuck with me as I learned what it meant. Through this man's persistent teaching, I learned and experienced the joy of seeing God work in my life. I finally was able to understand that I didn't have to be the rotten kid I always thought I was in the family of God. Because of my inability to control myself, I was always under the impression that I was accepted by Him due to a loophole in Scripture: "Whosoever will...(gulp)...and Karen...may come" (Rev. 22:17).

My sense that I was an afterthought in the eyes of God made me feel unable to have victory in my life. I felt like a pretender each time I raised my hand in Sunday school and worse than a liar when I sang in church. How could I share the joy of my salvation when I feared making eye contact with anyone who might see right through me? That belief changed dramatically when I finally understood the true meaning of patience, and that I had a choice when faced with people, places, or things that made me angry.

What Do We Do Now?

I discovered that the biggest hurdle most of us face is NOT that we're rebellious before God. Not deliberately, at least. We would gladly follow the Lord in doing what He wants us to do if He would only tell us exactly what it is.

Of concern is the acknowledgement that we don't know what we don't know. How can we make a wise decision with only partial information? I spent years being indecisive about whether I was smart enough or godly enough to obey the Lord's leading. It seemed as if everyone in my life had an opinion, yet no two opinions were alike. If each one was wiser or more discerning than I was, why were they so different from each other? And if they were all seeking God's will in my life as well as their own, how could the options appear to be so varied? Couldn't God make up His mind either?

In frustration I would jump to conclusions about the rules and regulations of being a believer, anticipate everyone's thoughts and motives before anything was stated, and try to solve or prevent interpersonal difficulties before they even appeared. This created many unnecessary conflicts as I assumed I knew what someone was thinking, and would react negatively to his or her every twitch and sigh.

And my story is similar to any believer who desires to know God's leading in his or her life. It's no wonder we become angry, frustrated and embarrassed when we discover our judgments have been based on inaccurate, incomplete information; thus our overreactions were stimulated by something we *thought* was true.

Let's Begin

So let me introduce you to "Lord, Shut Me Up!" hereafter referred to as LSMU. As I describe these concepts, keep in mind that "love" mentioned in these verses refers to God, our heavenly Father. We are to strive in our spiritual lives to be like Him (I John 3:2); therefore, as we read and learn more regarding these concepts, we must examine how well each of us displays these attributes:

- *Love (God) is patient*
- *Love (God) is kind*
- *It (He) does not envy*
- *It (He) does not boast*
- *It (He) is not proud*
- *It (He) is not rude*
- *It (He) is not self-seeking*
- *It (He) is slow to anger*
- *(God) Keeps not a record of wrongs*
- *(God) Does not delight in evil but rejoices with the truth*
- *It (He) protects*

- *(He) is trustworthy*

- *(He) brings hope*

- *(He) perseveres*

- *Love (God) never fails.*

I Corinthians 13:4–8a

Now You're in for It!

We are going to discuss and evaluate the concepts of patience and anger. The goal is to teach what you may not know. Be prepared to allow the Holy Spirit to reveal thoughts and attitudes you've relied on in the past that have not worked. I encourage you to be responsible for your actions and reactions so you may experience success in anger management. More than anything, my desire is that you may experience a stronger and more personal relationship with God with each successful response in this area of your life. Please be assured that you have unconditional safety through the shed blood of Christ as you allow Jesus to loosen the tightly clenched fingers that are grasped around your heart. You may tremble with trepidation, but the benefits of accepting His safety far outweigh the pain you've experienced through uncontrolled anger.

"I'm Not Worthy"

It's crucial that you understand that this information is not reserved for the "biggest and best" Christian in God's kingdom. "But grow in grace, and in the knowledge of our Lord and Savior Jesus Christ. To Him be glory both now and forever" (II Peter 3:18). There are no secret passwords or hidden codes so you may grow in grace and knowledge. It is simply the means by which all believers can take God at His Word, believing that He is Who He says He is,

and will do what He says He will do. There are no excep-
tions and no loopholes.

Temper Tantrums of the world, unite! Let this be the
beginning of your new life; the life that channels your
passions to fruitful undertakings. The life that relies thoroughly on the power of the Holy Spirit as you take responsibility for your anger and pray, "Lord, Shut Me Up!"

Two

Patience

Many Christians get their definition of patience from Sunday School class and church sermons. While learned biblical scholars still grapple with its full meaning, we believers attempt to capture its relevance to us and explain it in one short sentence.

As we explore our personal interpretation of patience, the responses tend to read like a fairy tale from ye olden days of wicked stepmothers and princesses who were protected by little birds and dwarfs—sounds good but not realistic or possible in our modern life:

- Endurance in suffering
- Bearing up under pressure without complaint
- Submitting to the demands of other individuals
- Waiting demurely

- Tolerating inappropriate behavior aimed at us personally

- Accepting leftovers after everyone else goes ahead of us

- Being last in line, not chosen to be on a team, "making do"

- And all the while having a good attitude about the entire situation.

The most common reference to patience is Job; in fact, the entire Old Testament book of Job relates the suffering endured by this man. We're grateful we don't have to experience what Job lived through (even though most of us are so stressed and over-extended that it sounds almost restful to have nothing to do but sit on an ash heap all day). Another example is the overworked person who longs for the flu so he or she can take the day off.

My clients often recite the usual definition of patience they think I want to hear. Each response echoes of self-sacrifice and blind obedience to God. However, as I persistently seek their true interpretation of patience, most admit that they aren't that comfortable with it. The concept is unfair and unreasonable. It may have worked in the "old days" but certainly doesn't apply to what our lives are like today.

It Doesn't Sound Good to Me

Patience implies that we are to allow ourselves to be taken advantage of and like it (or at least not complain where anyone can hear us). It flies in the face of American ideology that says that life must be fair. The customary definition of patience implies that we accept victimization without complaint because we're taught that God expects such an attitude from us. Yeah, and I also like getting poked in the eye.

The Oxford Definition of Patience:

"*n*. Perseverance, the ability to endure; forbearance." (p. 604)

Synonyms of Patience: tolerance, restraint, stoicism, fortitude, endurance, sufferance, submission, diligence, tenacity, doggedness, assiduity.

Along with the human definition of patience, there is also the Biblical reference in James 1:2–3:

"My brethren, count it all joy when ye fall into divers temptations;
    Knowing this, that the trying of your faith worketh patience."

When is the last time you encountered a major obstacle in your life that threatened to unhinge you completely? Did you interpret it as a joyful experience as you exclaimed to all within shouting distance, "Hallelujah, I'm growing in patience!"?

Get real

If you're like the rest of us, you were rocked back on your heels as you wondered what on earth you ever did to deserve such treatment. Such is the genuine response we have during trials; it is often well *after* the experience is behind us that we are able to acknowledge that God was working in and through it and we've grown because of it.

There is almost a superstition in Christian circles that implies that to request patience from God is to invite untold trouble into our lives. Sometimes to illustrate this response I challenge folks to approach someone in their church or Bible study and request a prayer for patience. Most report back that there was a sense of fear, hushed tones, and even sidelong glances to ensure that no one overheard the request!

This perception leads most of us to run, not walk, from even allowing ourselves to consider the value of this concept. Come on, why ask for trials when we often create our own, thank you very much.

I think that to pray for patience in this way is akin to being in junior high school and finding out that someone had placed a "KICK ME" sign on our backs. It is ridiculous to think that anyone would willingly make themselves a target for classmates (but it sure is funny when it happens to someone else…).

Requesting additional stresses and troubles in our lives just so we can practice not getting mad seems nuts.

But WAIT! There's More...

Patience is the act of purposely staying behind from the expected or what would be considered the normal thing to do (Luke 2:43), (Acts 17:14). It involves the willingness to suffer for a higher good than one's own self-gratification (Romans 8:24), (I Peter 2:20).

The word *patience* (*hupomeno* in Greek) leads us to *long-suffering* (*makrothumeo* in Greek):

> To be long-spirited, forbearing or patient bear (suffer) long, be longsuffering, have (long) patience, be patient, patiently endure.

> Long-suffering is that quality of self-restraint in the face of provocation which does not hastily retaliate or promptly punish; it is the opposite of anger, and

is associated with mercy, and is used of God, Exodus 34:6, Romans 2:4; I Peter 3:20. Patience is the quality that does not surrender to circumstances or succumb under trial; it is the opposite of despondency and is associated with hope (I Thessalonians 1:3).

The genuine meaning of patience is to wait upon God for an answer to a situation before acting. It means to deliberately remain, to stick with the situation, to learn all the facts. It is the act of purposefully staying behind, which is not the expected or the normal thing to do. In short, to show patience is to hang in there until the situation is fully revealed, and to exhibit self control in the meantime.

Imagine that someone is hanging off the side of a burning building desperately waiting for the firemen to guide the large truck ladder up to rescue him. Common sense would assume that the need to remain exactly where he is would be the safest place for him. What if he decided he'd waited long enough and simply let go? He would have plenty of time to complain about his discomfort while recuperating in the hospital…we hope.

Our Reaction to Conflict

Our reaction to conflict will often affect how we utilize patience. Most believers are convinced that any kind of disagreement between themselves and someone else is ungodly; they assume that differences of opinions are death knells to spiritual growth and that any discomfort is wrong. Thus they do whatever is necessary to ignore or elude the conflict: shutting down and curling up into an emotional fetal position; the body is there but no one is home.

"If I Close My Eyes, Maybe You'll Go Away"

This is what I call *hibernation*, which is the tendency to go to sleep mentally, emotionally, or spiritually, and float off into a form of disassociation. This disassociation seems more likely to be believed in an exciting psychological thriller one would pay to see at a theater. But truthfully, many forms of hibernation occur regularly in our homes today:

—Dad senses conflict so he buries himself in his work, his hobbies, or his sports teams.

—Mom hides behind her day planner, her children's activities, and church responsibilities.

—The kids respond in kind, staying in their rooms buried in homework, cell phones, or video games.

Hibernation is a survival technique that creates no new conflict and makes no waves. As attractive as that sounds, it serves no purpose but to lose time. Individuals who use this method to survive conflict are only putting off an inescapable interaction since the factors will still have to be addressed at a later date. There is no learning or growing with hibernation and anyone in conflict with these folks grows even more aggressive when they observe no satisfactory reaction. Their mission then becomes not only the desire to win the argument, but also to get some response even if it is negative. The lack of reaction is interpreted as a deliberate failure to respect or show courtesy to the one causing the conflict. The issue is now complicated by the perceived failure to listen to, or care about, a differing opinion.

The Best Defense Is a Good Offense

Overreaction is the other reaction to conflict, especially among those of us with short fuses. We rely on old memories and experiences in our interpretation of current events and think we are seeing the big picture of a situation as we jump into the middle of it. We claim we are only being truthful and that it's not our fault if someone takes offense at our actions. We quote that Jesus cast the moneychangers out of the temple (Matt. 21:12) so He could be a tough guy and still be on track spiritually. We claim we are "speaking the truth in love" but in reality there is no love involved.

Getting the Big Picture about Little Things

The ironic fact about conflict is that it often starts with inconsequential things: Wet towels on the floor, lost car keys, uncharged cell phones, missing remote controls. The conflict escalates to the point where it becomes less about the issue and more about who's going to win. Often, the person who wins the battle is NOT the one who is right, but rather the one who yells the loudest! Now the other party is not only resentful because of the primary issue, but also because he or she was out-yelled. This causes a rift that may heal over time, but is very fragile, until the next conflict when the old hurt is added to the new disagreement. Thus, the issue gets blown out of proportion and some future argument that begins small, explodes for no apparent reason. This leaves behind a sense of wondering, what on earth just happened?

When we remodeled our basement to provide a bedroom for our then-teenaged daughter Kari, we ended up putting more electrical outlets in one corner of our house. This worked well until one day everyone decided to use a radio, blow dryer, or curling iron at the same time. An electrical overload was created that blew a fuse. From that time on we found that the circuitry was weakened, and using even fewer appliances would send us scrambling to the fuse box.

The same thing is true when conflict is smoothed over instead of dealt with; it takes much less "electricity" each time to create an argument. Even a glance or a sigh can be enough to cause a "circuitry overload."

These conflict behaviors serve to create a sense of unease among those of us who experience it on a regular basis. Even worse, should the recent conflict fail to be addressed between the individuals involved, the perceived lack of safety and concern can create a sense of fear and mistrust between them. It can be described as a sense of discomfort and unpredictability that enslaves us and those we love. Because we are uncomfortable and frustrated we flare up over every incident, however inconsequential. We react to the often normal behaviors of others, and find ourselves watching their tics and twitches rather than being responsible for ourselves (Matt. 7:3–5), (Lk. 6:41, 42). Then we claim that we misbehaved because of what someone else said or did instead of simply admitting that we were wrong. Finally, when we do admit that we were a jerk, we feel so guilty we hesitate to repent before God because we have committed this sin so often.

So, what can we do about it? We could stay in this cycle of behavior because it is familiar and, in a weird way, comfortable. It's what we know. (It seems easier to remain clueless about my actions; otherwise I have to suffer guilt and conviction if I own up to what I have done.) Since we know no other way to deal with anger, we often believe we are stuck experiencing the same pain on a continual basis. Therefore, our family members and friends must also be subjected to our inappropriate actions.

But there is more to godly living than keeping our eyes averted and our hands covering our ears. We are meant to know, and be known by others and God, in a real, practical, and honest way.

Admit it!

It is critical to understand and accept that any spiritual and behavioral change in our lives must begin with taking responsibility for our own ability (or inability) to handle conflict. We bring into each interaction an entire grab bag of past experiences that seems to confirm our assertion that we're right and everyone else is wrong. Yet judging from the suffering we experience and inflict, we know that can't be entirely true. For that reason, we will begin to honestly examine and discard the useless attitudes and actions that prevent us from enjoying peace and contentment even when in conflict.

THREE

Anger

How many times do we hear these comments:

"If it wasn't for _____ I wouldn't have gotten mad."

"_____ is a jerk and it isn't fair."

"I was fine until she_____."

"I had one last nerve and he stepped on it."

Isn't it amazing how it always seems as if some special circumstance causes us to lose our composure? We excuse our inappropriate behavior by blaming someone or something else; it's rarely acknowledged that we simply got mad and blew it. We don't sit in a room by ourselves thinking happy thoughts when, out of nowhere, anger comes along and beans us upside the head.

No way, my friend!

Thought-Opinion-Judgment

We sit and think about a situation that we are dealing with currently or have just recently experienced. Fine, because it is just *a thought*, we could just as well be thinking about what we had for lunch three weeks ago for all the effect it has on us.

What gets us in trouble is when we carry the thought further and allow ourselves an *opinion* about it. Then we determine that we either liked or disliked that situation, which brings us to the last step which is the most dangerous: *judgment*.

First there is the thought, then the opinion, and then the judgment that something is wrong or unfair about the outcome. We get mad. We heat up. We explode. The situation is not okay with us and we are determined to stand up for ourselves. At stake is the fear that our "rights" have been violated. We are convinced that we must defend our position to prove we have value; that what we say matters even if it makes no sense to anyone else. We do and say whatever is necessary to win the battle, despite the scars we inflict and the messes we might have to clean up afterward.

Ultimately, our reaction to whatever triggered the anger is almost always far more extreme than the event itself. It has the ability to transform a small sense of discomfort into a full-blown temper tantrum. Maybe not a physical tantrum, with its kicking and screaming and rolling around on the floor; perhaps more like a verbal onslaught that thrashes and smashes the hearts and feelings of everyone who has the misfortune of being in its path.

Remember my nickname in grade school? I wasn't dubbed "Temper Tantrum" without reason. I remember the intensity of my wrath and the frustration of not being able to express myself appropriately. So I'd literally throw myself on the floor and kick and yell and slam my fists into the woodwork until I was exhausted. But you know what? I discovered one annoying fact after launching a massive temper tantrum that we still encounter in our rage today: eventually we all have to pick ourselves up off the floor! And believe me it's embarrassing, pointless, and worthless in the grand scheme of what it was that brought you to such an emotional conclusion: a thought that turned into an opinion, which then became a judgment.

Me? Argue with God?

What we overlook is what we're really insinuating when we make this judgment call: that ultimately God must have made a mistake by letting whatever occurred get by Him. He must have been napping, right? He was probably busy dealing with floods or earthquakes and just let it slip by Him, but *we* won't. We'll catch it and pass judgment and even make the transgressor pay for his or her sins for a long while afterwards.

Angry Christians initially protest against any suggestion that God messed up in this circumstance. But when the attitude and behavior is followed to its logical conclusion, they reluctantly agree that although that was certainly not their intention, it sure must look like that to God.

Sit and think for a minute about the last time you lost your composure. I recently experienced this myself when celebrating Christmas with my family.

We have the tradition that on Christmas Day, after the stockings have been emptied and we've puttered around with our gifts (and I've snagged and made sure to lick everyone's peppermint sticks), we play bingo. It's a fun tradition that involves making the rules up as you go along and choosing a gaily-wrapped mystery gift if you win a game. After the gifts are all won, we are then allowed to steal each others' gifts with no remorse or recrimination.

As usual, I was the last one to settle down to play the game and I was getting irritated from being pushed to hurry. I found myself spouting spiteful comments under my breath to show my displeasure.

It was then that my son Ryan said, "LSMU, Mom."

How dare my child use my own teachings against me! After my initial sense of outrage, I had to admit that it was my thought ("they're really pushing me") that slid into an opinion ("it's not right; can't they see I still have stuff to do first?") that became a judgment ("they're selfish and I'm not being appreciated").

If I'm Right...

By the time we focus on judgment our thoughts have turned inward; our perception is that any opinion different from our own is a threat to us. We then either shut down in the conflict (hibernate) or forcefully push away (overreact) as we respond to the belief that we have to do whatever is necessary to win in order to survive. The other person then becomes an opponent and all bets are off—if I'm a "good guy" then he must by necessity become the "bad guy." We attribute hugely negative motives to that person or persons.

I often laughingly confide to clients that we give the person with whom we're in conflict way too much credit. When I'm angry at my husband, I'm convinced that he has spent many long hours scheming to find ways to aggravate me. Actually, he's merely expressing the fact that he doesn't really care for my choice of where to go for our next vacation! Many of us have the same attitude, wasting so much time and energy obsessing about the thoughts and motives of others.

Who's REALLY Being Hurt?

When Don and I were still young parents, we worked closely with another couple from our church. Logically, we should have found so many things in common; we were close in age, had graduated from the same Bible college, and even lived in the same neighborhood. Due to these similarities, it was only natural that the wife and I spent long hours together in person or on the phone as we both stayed home with our babies.

It wasn't long before I noticed several habits this woman had that really irritated me.

She exhibited attitudes that I, as a newer Christian, felt she shouldn't have (read: "get away with"). I'd try to confront her about these tendencies but to no avail; I'm sure that my motives behind these confrontations were selfish and so these interactions were usually unsatisfying. I found myself thinking about her all the time, watching for her to mess up and hoping she'd be humbled before God (and hopefully a VERY large group of onlookers!).

It never happened. After seven years of ministering there, my family relocated to another state where I not only unpacked my kids and luggage, but my negative opinion of this woman as well.

It was bad, I must admit. I know from personal experience how fertile our imaginations can be in the wee hours of the morning. How eloquent and brave I was! How forceful and upright! Then I'd roll over and fall asleep, only to forget what fabulous statements I was going to make to her if the opportunity ever arose.

I finally realized how pointless it was to waste my time clinging to an anger I could not resolve personally; I had to go through my own spiritual and emotional housecleaning so I could reestablish my right standing with God.

Once I did so, I came to a startling realization: I had spent countless hours obsessing over someone else's behavior. Yet in those seven years of anger and sleepless nights, that woman had never lost one second of sleep over me! Then a quote I'd heard somewhere came to my mind:

"Bitterness (anger) is like swallowing rat poison and waiting for the other person to die."

That was me! I was dying both spiritually and emotionally due to anger and bitterness about something over which I had no control. Meanwhile I waited (with "baited" breath?) for her to suffer for something she wasn't even aware she had done.

Okay, Now I'm Listening

I had to confess before God that I had been guilty of being judge and jury to this woman. But what I really was insinuating all those seven years was that God was not doing His job! By griping and moping around, by examining this gal's flaws, I was showing God that if it were up to me I'd have done things differently. Old comments I had spoken echoed in my heart, such as "It's a good thing I'm not God or (insert name here) would be a crispy critter." Or, "I wouldn't allow that if it were me." At the time the statements were made, my motive was to judge the *other* person. But in my hours of sharing these concepts since then, and revealing my own attitudes concerning them, I've come to realize that I was unwittingly inferring that God was failing me. I had been critical of someone else's unspiritual behavior and discovered I had been equally (if not even *more*) unrighteous before my Heavenly Father.

"Here, Mousey Mousey Mousey..."

Does this sound familiar to you? Do you find yourself watching the actions of someone else, rating their value only to find them lacking? Do you carry an emotional box of rat poison around with you to the point that its effects permeate your every thought? This is what influences how often you lose your temper and creates a sense of condemnation towards yourself and your intended target.

"Won't Somebody Feel Sorry For Me?"

On the other hand, some individuals seem to enjoy being miserable. These folks tend to find their identity in obsessing about how wronged they have been in their lives and what they *could* have been if only they hadn't been mistreated in some way. This victim mentality initially seems well-founded. We want to protect and defend these dear ones, often becoming angry for their plight and wanting to get involved.

But I've noticed over time that these people seldom grow or change. Perhaps they are blinded to their habitual victimization and would truly love the freedom only God can provide. Perhaps their spiritual growth is deliberately stunted because it sometimes feels really good to have others care and show indignation over their plight.

Personal responsibility is vital to healing. The desire to accept that our thoughts and attitudes need changing is the first positive step in anger management; God will give us the ability if we truly want it and are willing to act on what we learn.

I began my foray into Christian counseling as a client, and this very issue is what made me realize that I needed help. I needed to understand that God was personally interested in me and loved me for who I currently was rather than who I was working so hard to become. I finally realized that each day I lived was a treasure and it was up to me how I was going to spend it. Do I waste it with reactive/angry living or do I let God be God?

In my efforts to understand how to quit gulping down the rat poison, I asked the Holy Spirit to give me a helpful illustration. As I closed my eyes I imagined my life was over and I was standing before God in heaven. He was seated on His glorious throne and a huge throng of glowing angels were gathered around Him on either side.

I timidly approached God at His bidding and He gently asked me, "Karen, I must ask you: why did you do the things you did while on Earth?"

In a pitiful voice I replied, "My husband made me angry and my kids tried my patience. My church friends were jerks and I was misunderstood."

Then God kindly looked to His right and to His left, slowly and deliberately. Then He finally returned His gaze to me.

"I don't see them here right now. So again I repeat the question: Why did *you* do the things you did while on earth?"

As I opened my eyes I finally understood—No matter what anyone else said or did in my entire lifetime, no matter what its effect has been on me, I was the one who would ultimately have to answer for my behavior. No excuses or rationalizations would suffice; I would not be able to hide behind anyone else when I finally stood before God.

This was earth shattering to me; alert the media! I realized that if that is the case, I want to be fully responsible for any decisions I make or responses I give to others in my life.

That's when I made up a little catchphrase I'd like to share with you:

INU2Y: IT'S NOT UP 2 YOU!

This phrase is a mental reminder that we are free to make our own choices, to live peacefully before God daily. "It's Not Up 2 You" is a catchphrase intended to remind us that as we deal with meaningful people in our lives, we still have to make, and be responsible for, our choices in life. It is intended to be an internal statement made to the other person as our personal choices are reclaimed. Despite the varying opinions voiced by those for whom we care deeply, we must be able to look at them and decide, "INU2Y."

The intention is not to be disrespectful to someone's suggestions, nor is it an excuse to disregard the thoughts and wishes of our loved ones (or even the folks we don't like!). It is meant to serve as a reminder of the freedom we have been given as redeemed children of God. As we finally stand before God, the goal is to have peace that each of life's decisions on earth was not made at the insistence of someone else.

INU2Y is also meant to instill a sense of personal responsibility that keeps us accountable for our behavior. As much as a boss or coworker is a jerk to us, we are still liable for our attitudes. If another church member hurts us and causes strife in the family of God, we still can choose our course of action according to what Scripture, rather than our emotions, tells us to do.

Even when there is true injury done to us we can use INU2Y to remind us that we can choose to not allow it to have power over who we truly are in Christ.

Not too long ago I decided to focus on INU2Y and had

small buttons made to give to my clients and anyone who attended my LSMU classes. Before long I was seeing those little tokens being flashed proudly on lapels and purses everywhere. It was exciting to see how God could turn a few simple words into a crucial tool. I've even had men reach into their pockets and show a button intermingled with their pocket change. It showed me how excited people were to realize they could live honestly before God and the joy they felt in having a choice.

A Sharp Little Visual Aid

The point is, God gives us tools to aid us in our quest for utter dependence on Him; we don't need to have everything stored in our heads. I, for one, need little spiritual post-it notes to help me and I'm sure I'm not alone.

Another concept with INU2Y is that it allows you to take your eyes off horizontal situations and turn them vertically to God where they belong.

We tend to check the opinions of many people in our lives before we're able to make a decision; it seems that over time we surrender our ability to pick and choose wisely. From hairstyles to prospective mates, we check and double check with everyone we've ever met over the pros and cons of what's going on in our lives. Then, if something goes wrong with that decision, we get even more confused. After all, the majority is always right, *right*?

Wrong. INU2Y reminds us that, although it is wise to confide in a few trustworthy loved ones, ultimately WE are the ones who will have to live with the decisions we make.

It can be difficult to disengage yourself from the entanglement of sharing your opinion of what a friend does in his or her life. It's flattering to be consulted, and we find ourselves enmeshed in the drama as it is retold to us secondhand. During this time, INU2Y is a vital helper when you need to step away: remember, INU2Y either!

It feels heartless to tell someone that they need to make their own choices and it's none of your business. I've repeated this many times over the course of my career "It's not up to me, Friend. What do you feel God wants *you* to do? See, I could give you all kinds of wisdom and advice, tell you to leave the loser or stay. Drop the crummy job or hang tight. Go to a different church that appreciates you or stick with this one. But you're the one who will have to live with the choices you make—when I leave here tonight I'm going home to my family, and honestly I won't be thinking about you.

So whatever you decide has to be your own choice."

Back to Anger

This leads us back to the beginning: anger that begins as a thought, becomes an opinion, then dissolves into judgment. There is a choice here, too. All anger is our decision; sometimes the decision is made for us if the situation is obviously against what is taught in Scripture. We are not to do anything that contradicts God's Word.

But the other cases are certainly up to us. Therefore, it is imperative that we use wisdom in order to gain insight into our identity before God, and to recognize His leading in our daily lives.

Four

Pride

Of all the negative traits I admit to having possessed in my life, pride would not be one of them. Proud of what? I'd not had a sense of accomplishment, of success, of exhibiting much poise or grace under fire. My personal attributes were average and my relationships were limited. On a human scale, it seemed as if my inferiority excluded me from being guilty of pride.

The Oxford Dictionary defines pride as "a high or overbearing opinion of one's worth or importance. Self-satisfaction, conceit, proudness (is that a real word or must I look it up?), egotism, egocentricity, self-importance, haughtiness, vanity, arrogance, overconfidence, self-love, smugness."

Despite these descriptors, it isn't necessary to think one is wonderful to exhibit pride. Pride presents itself in most believers as self-preservation; the result of fear; being afraid of giving in, giving up, being taken advantage of, not being respected or heard. Pride rears its ugly head when we feel we've given too much and are not being appreciated.

Listen in on most church hospitality groups after a meeting:

"I can't believe Louise refused to have me bake my prize winning pie for the Ladies Tea! With all I do..."

"Well! You'd think Jane would be happy for my husband's promotion and bonus and the money we can now use to further God's work. After all, her husband's been out of work for almost a year now. At least *someone* can afford to offer to purchase new wallpaper for the nursery, even if she can't."

Pride displays itself as unrighteousness hidden behind a mask of righteousness. It can be simmered down to its most basic premise: I'm going to do what I want, no matter how I have to word it to make it sound palatable.

Several years ago I spoke on the phone with the head of a local Christian counseling agency. Matt was pleasant and agreeable, yet something about his conversation made me feel uncomfortable. No, he wasn't inappropriate to me nor did he disrespect me in any way. However, as our conversation progressed, I noticed a theme; whenever the subject broached on possible roadblocks or concerns, he laughingly stated, "I don't go over obstacles; I go through them." In a ten-minute phone call Matt made that assertion three times.

Ending the call, I mused over his words for a long time until it struck me: Pride.

"I don't go over obstacles; I go through them." He was

so pleased with what he defined as determination to do God's will. But suppose God had provided the obstacles to get him to wait for His direction?

What Happens When You Assume?

Pride is independent thinking apart from God and/or the unwillingness to be submissive to God before reacting. Pride is a distorted sense of reality in which assumption plays a large part, much like squinting through a hole in the fence and believing you see the whole elephant.

How many times have you entered a roomful of people only to have them stop in mid-sentence to look at you? Did you assume they were talking about you? Were you left wondering if you'd forgotten to put on an article of clothing before going out, or thought perhaps you had broccoli stuck in your teeth? How about being convinced that someone's facial expression or offhand comment is aimed solely at you?

Many of us have experienced the embarrassment of interpreting a situation and acting on that interpretation, only to later discover our facts were wrong. It's like trying to navigate around an unfamiliar room with our eyes shut; we can guarantee at least a few bumps and bruises along the way.

Something about being in conflict brings out the worst in us—we seldom stay focused during the interaction to hear and see it all. No, the majority of us either run away from it or run smack dab into it! Our emotions limit our common sense, giving us a skewed picture of what's really happening. Then we act according to what we *thought* we saw (or he said, or she did), often creating *more* conflict in the process. I must confess to quite a few instances where I came upon my kids in mid argument, made a snap decision and punished the wrong one. Of course, they would say I did it more often than I will admit to. But maybe that's just my pride…

Behaviors Showing Pride

Independence from God is the basic form of pride as described in Luke 12:16–21 (NIV):

> And he spake a parable unto them, saying, The ground of a certain rich man brought forth plentifully; And he thought within himself, saying, What shall I do, because I have no room where to bestow my fruits? And he said, This will I do: I will pull down my barns, and build greater; and there will I bestow all my fruits and my goods. And I will say to my soul, Soul, thou hast much goods laid up for many years; take thine ease, eat, drink, and be merry. But God said unto him, Thou fool, this night thy soul shall be required of thee; then whose shall those things be, which thou hast provided? So is he that layeth up treasure for himself, and is not rich toward God.

The rich man in this parable mistakenly believed he could live by his own rules and credit his wealth to his own efforts. Prideful independence averted his focus from God; rather, he gave himself the credit for his success.

No matter what the circumstances, pride causes us to fiercely fight anyone at any time to win the argument. When the contest is at its apex, we hit our opponent with whatever verbal weapon we have no matter how damaging the blow. Pride blinds us from identifying our target; when the dust clears we are horrified to see that someone we love dearly has been caught in our crossfire. Then we become hypocritical medics forced to tend to the wounds of our own victims. Not so "friendly fire."

I Timothy 6:4 in the Amplified Bible states:

> He is puffed up with pride and stupefied with con-
> ceit, [although he is] woefully ignorant. He has a
> morbid fondness for controversy and disputes and
> strife about words, which result in (produce) envy
> and jealousy, quarrels and dissension, abuse and in-
> sults and slander, and base suspicions.

"Let's Have a Clean Fight"

In my experience as a counselor I have witnessed interactions between people who make me wonder if I'm a Su-
preme Court judge or a referee. Most conversations center
around who said what to whom:

"You told me you'd mow the lawn last weekend."

"Did not."

"Did too."

"Did not."

"Did too."

"Well, you told *me* you'd wash the car."

"Did not."

"Did too."

"Did not."

"Did too."

Then it gets more heated:

"If you had done what you were supposed to do, then
I'd have done what I was supposed to do."

"I couldn't do what I was supposed to do because I
didn't know what it was I was supposed to do."

"That's not true! You knew what I wanted you to do.
We talked about it on the way home from church. You're
a liar!"

"I'm not lying. I knew you'd try to push me around, so
I didn't say *anything* when you asked me to help you."

By this time my head is lying on my arms on my desk as I react to this angry and prideful interchange between two individuals who have claimed to love and honor each other.

Yet here they are, bickering over what was and wasn't stated during a prior conversation.

Just recently, a dear woman named Dani shared her personal frustration with a man she knew who suffers from pride. Upon telling Dani that he was married, he'd admitted to her that he'd had an extramarital affair but he and his wife were "cool." After being pressed on the issue, he denied lying to his wife; saying she just didn't ask the right questions.

Almost akin to a political debate, the decision over who has the best case rests more on what was *not* said than on what *was* stated. Pride manipulates our very vocabulary, leaving out valuable facts in order to appear cooperative but still hold the trump card. Known as the "sin of omission," it is a subtle tool used by angry and resentful people as a means to lure another person into a belief that all is well.

You Have to Read Between the Lines

Pride is also evidenced when we distort reality to be better than we are, or to win an argument. "Always" and "Never" are clever weapons in this altercation.

"I *Always* put down the toilet seat."

"I *never* get to do what I want to do."

"You *always* think you're right."

"You *never* admit when you're wrong."

There can also be a misuse of Scripture to manipulate and appear more spiritual than someone else. The most commonly misused portions of Scripture are those that center around the husband and wife relationship (Ephesians 5:22–24), (Hebrews. 13:4), (Deuteronomy 22:5), (I Corinthians 14:35). To my wry amusement, I have noticed that many proud verse-quoting persons seldom read anything else in the Bible, nor do they attend local services to gain credibility to argue such spiritual issues.

Watch Where You're Stepping...

Proverbs 16:18 (NIV):

> "Pride goes before destruction, and a haughty spirit before a fall."

The level of independence from God determines how willing we are to surrender our pride in a conflict. Our decision to submit to God will strengthen us as we step back; it is crucial that we seek Him and admit we could actually be wrong.

The problem with pride is that we can make it sound so good. Scores of friends and family can listen to your side of the story (which gets more creative with each telling) and agree that you were justified in your behavior. But they go on with their lives and their relationships, leaving you to live with the consequences of what was said or done. At that point an honest self-evaluation is long overdue, and here is the question to ask:

"Do I want to enjoy relationships...or be *right* all by myself?"

Lest that sound like allowing victimization and mistreatment by others so that a relationship may be maintained, let me explain further. In no way should abuse or degradation be allowed so that we might avoid loneliness. As redeemed children of God, we should expect to be treated in a respectful manner. That is not the issue here.

The focus on this statement is whether the need to carry on the argument without compromise is so strong it creates distance between you and the other person.

Wounded individuals feel that their loved one isn't even willing to listen to their side of the story. Being shut down from having an opinion, or an opportunity for discussion, creates a wall that is difficult to climb without help. If this continues time after time the relationship is in real trouble.

Catch the Catch Phrases

Of note is the fact that prideful attitudes influence prideful speech. Despite the acknowledgement that the words will most likely be hurtful, a proud person will say them anyway—only they preface it with a disclaimer:

"I don't want to hurt your feelings but…"

"Don't take this the wrong way but…"

"I know you're not going to like this but…"

And here's my favorite disclaimer of all:

"Promise me that what I'm about to tell you won't make you mad."

Talk about distortion! The position taken by the prideful person is now, "You've been warned…you can't get mad, hurt, or aggravated because I told you it might be a problem before I even said it." Notice how suddenly you've become the bad guy?

Now be honest, who wouldn't feel anxious thinking that something was going on that they didn't know about, especially if it concerns them? Of course then they will insist they can handle it and won't freak out or get upset just so they can hear what it is.

Here's a helpful tip to use the next time any of those phrases are said to you:

Just when the person gets to the "but" portion of the sentence, interrupt and say, "Then DON'T." It throws off the dynamic and in all probability makes the speaker step back and think it through. Then if he insists on trying to tell you anyway, you can reply:

"Why would you want to tell me something that might upset me? That doesn't seem very _____(fill in the blank with the appropriate word, i.e. thoughtful, friendly, helpful, considerate, godly)."

ME First!

Unrepentant pride can be the factor that damages families; spouses and children experience frustration and irritation when being repeatedly rebuffed by stubborn responses such as, "that's just the way I am," or "get over it." These statements may be justification for having said the wrong thing or having the wrong attitude, but the words are often interpreted as, "I'm more important than you are," "I don't care how much I just hurt you," "I will say what I want to say no matter what."

I've seen big burly men fight back tears as they hear their wives admit anger and resentment as a result of their prideful words. Never would these fellas have dreamed that what they thought was an offhand comment could cause so much damage to a relationship. It's not a matter of an unwillingness to accept imperfection; anyone who is married (or has been married, or will be married, or knows someone who is married!) understands that everyone makes errors in judgment and can cause pain (like when my husband tries to dance with me while wearing his wing-tipped church shoes...now *that's* pain!). The difficulty arises when pride pushes people away and takes away their right to express disagreement or a differing viewpoint, thus creating insecurity in the relationship.

Rebellion toward Authority

Remember my early years? My temper got me into so much trouble, but I must confess that while my temper was the vehicle, I was the driver. And I was like Jehu in the Old Testament book II Kings 9:20 (NIV): "...driving furiously." Read the passage; Jehu appears to have been the first speeding fatality!

My earliest memories are of not wanting to be obedient. No matter what the activity, I didn't want to do it. Why? Because it wasn't my idea. If I'd thought of it first and decided it would be a good thing to do, I'd be very cooperative. But if someone else beat me to it, I would reject it outright.

As I grew into adolescence, I became even prouder of my own choices and their results. I just knew that whatever I decided to do had to be done my way. And woe to anyone who had a different idea! This attitude came to a blistering halt one day as a major disagreement taught me a painful lesson.

No One's Going to Boss Me Around

At the point of this crisis my brothers had grown up and moved away, so it was just Mom and me at home most days. I was a messy teenager since I spent much of my time in my room moving from project to project without

putting any of them away. Every dresser, chair, bed, and
night stand was covered in whatever it is teenage girls collect.

It got to the point it was even bothering *me* so I determined that I was going to spend the day sorting it out and
cleaning it up. On my way to the kitchen to gather some
trash bags and cleaning supplies, Mom caught up with
me. "Karen, I'd like you to clean your room."

That was all I needed to hear—the pride reared up
and anger held the reins as I stomped off to my room in a
rage. I was livid.

Have you ever encountered something that riled up
your imagination to the strangest thoughts and plans? The
"I should…and that'll show her" thoughts that you know
deep in your heart you would never have the energy or
courage to do?

Well, I had the thought and I did it: I decided in my
rebelliousness that I would clean my room so well that my
mom would regret ever telling me to do it. I began cleaning with a vengeance, taking every possession I had and
stuffing, shoving, cramming, and packing them in hidden
places in my room; under my bed, in my closet, drawers,
and cupboards until not a single item could be seen. I even
took the curtains off my windows! It resembled a cloister
cell when I was done. Only my bed and a bare mattress
were evident.

Rage was still propelling me as I smugly surveyed my
room and called my mom from the other room to check
my handiwork. I would show her that I was not to be or-
dered around. I was proud of my creativity as I pompous-
ly opened my bedroom door to display what clean looked
like.

But what happened next brought me to my senses in a
way that even now I ache when I remember it. Instead of

Mom turning to me and waving a white flag in surrender to my superior fighting skills, she did something I never expected: she cried.

In the skewed perspective of pride and immaturity, I had upped the ante so high that in order to win I had to resort to using my deadliest arsenal. My attitude slashed and scarred the one person in my life who meant the most to me.

Mom tearfully left the house and I was alone in the room that just a few minutes earlier had been a source of self-satisfaction. Not only was my bedroom stripped bare of artifice, so was I; in the echo of those empty walls, I felt my pride and arrogance crumble as I realized the damage I had done.

My tears and repentance could not repair the damage I had done to my mom. As I set out to restore my room to its proper order, I also had to allow God to restore my heart.

It took more than two days to get my bedroom set to rights, but even now the regret and pain I feel as I recall it so many years later cannot be forgotten.

So it is with pride when it is left unexamined. My example reflects the "I want what I want when I want it" perspective. Before you burn rubber (and your bridges) feeling angry at God and your circumstances, allow the Holy Spirit to examine your heart. Perhaps your anger has less to do with the behaviors of others and more to do with you.

FIVE

Rudeness

Personally and professionally, the most prevalent behavior I witness is rudeness. Not the run of the mill sticking-your-tongue-out or saying-inappropriate-things rudeness, but rather the subtle, often undetectable actions-that-would-almost-pass-unnoticed rudeness that makes you angry without understanding why.

We are very creative. How else can we explain our tendency to find ways to poke and prod those with whom we have grievances and then hide behind false innocence? We communicate disapproval by simply rolling our eyes or folding our arms. We mutter under our breaths and, when asked to repeat the comment, deny saying anything. Don't get me started on the art of the silent treatment! Many a worthy opponent has cowed under a well-executed stare down.

Rudeness is an expression of anger; while overt anger is right there in your face, rudeness is sneaky and manipulative. It is a form of attack that leaves the victim unaware of the assault until well after the situation.

You Talking to Me?

Rudeness is the absence of protection. It is exposing another's weakness and mocking them, then acting as if you didn't know that what you were doing was harmful.

It is known as "feigned ignorance" or pretending you don't know what you said when in reality you really were very aware of your words and actions. Rudeness can be masked behind sarcasm or cutting remarks. Angry statements can then be made and defended by responding that you were "only kidding."

Most of us are quick to explain that the negative comments we make toward ourselves or someone else are harmless; no one is physically injured. But how true is that assertion?

Think back to a time someone made a sarcastic comment to you or about you. Do you recall how you felt physically and emotionally?

I remember my dad telling me in fifth grade that I was getting tubby. I remember a friend of my step-dad asking me in a joking manner, "what made me think you could sing?"

I find it remarkable that I don't remember the positive things that were probably spoken about me at that time, but I certainly remember that someone thought I was fat and had no singing talent.

If you can recall a situation similar to mine, you have been the victim of rudeness. Comments that are uncomplimentary or hidden behind humor are prime examples.

View any current sitcom on television and you will observe rudeness in its purest form. Snide comments followed by a laugh track, disrespectful facial expressions and inappropriate body language assault our eyes and ears daily. Gentle humor is passé, cutting humor is in vogue. It is so prevalent that it has become the backbone of our communication style. And it can hurt because rudeness has a basis in truth; it's our way of saying what we really mean.

In junior high and high school, I discovered the girls' locker room to be a sure place to experience rudeness. I've heard that guys are ruthless, but listen in on any gaggle of adolescent girls who have zeroed in on some unfortunate loner who doesn't quite measure up.

Never mind reality shows depicting coalitions and cliques and verbal maneuvering; we females are geared to have double and even triple meanings behind every comment or facial expression.

We use those comments to express our dominance, anger, and impatience with others; we are aware that we can say anything to anyone so long as we say it with a smile.

On the other hand, it explains why many people are easily angered when interacting with someone else.

"I can't believe she said that!"

"What? She just said she liked our new puppy."

"That's not what she really said. She's obviously a cat person."

"Huh?"

"Oh, honey, you're so dim sometimes. She's got a white cat hair on her sweater, which means she likes cats. If she had a dog, she'd have dog hair on her. Besides that, she wasn't looking at the puppy when she said it, she was looking at you. Not me, *you*."

"So?"

"So? Don't tell me you didn't notice. The way she looked at you was disgraceful! And she's a married woman!"

"What? I think she and Frank are doing fine in their marriage…"

"That's what she *wants* everyone to think! That's why she mentioned the dog rather than something more personal. And you fell for it. You are so clueless."

Allow me to focus on the male perspective for a moment. I have often been amazed at the accuracy of the statement, "He looks married."

What does *married* look like? But having been privy to many arguments similar to the one above, I suspect there is one common element married men share. They all have a bewildered expression on their faces—"did you get the license plate of the bus that hit me?" It's from long term exposure to the feminine rationale of using feigned ignorance in dealings with themselves and others.

It is so common to encounter rudeness that we can become desensitized to it. After all, if you hear a sound often enough, after time it can be tuned out (like living by a train track, or a humming refrigerator, or a nagging teenager…).

But there are several cue sentences that might provide a clue when rudeness is present:

"I'm just kidding"

No matter the context of the prior statement, "I'm just kidding" is a protective shield that attempts to discount the damage done by the rude comment. It attempts to render powerless the defensive response triggered by the comment.

"Lighten up"

The person making the statement bounces it back and it is now the victim's fault, as if the offended were to blame rather than the offender.

"Can't you take a joke?"

Sure, if the joke wasn't at someone else's expense.

Insecurity

One common cause of rudeness is insecurity. We've all heard the saying "misery loves company." A popular saying when I was a kid was that if you wanted to appear thin, stand next to a heavier person. Most of us have been told by our well-meaning mommas, "They're just jealous of you." I'd think, "Whatever they want of mine they can have if they just quit bugging me."

Those soothing words are small comfort at the time. But it might be somewhat true.

When there is a sense of inequity, real or imagined, it becomes vital to level the playing field by any means possible.

I'll never forget a comment a coworker made years ago. Lorraine had spent much of her time insisting that women shouldn't wear pants; staff wives had to maintain the dress code, it wasn't biblical, and so on. Should some unsuspecting woman stray from that standard, Lorraine made it very clear (to me, not the offender!) that it was not permitted. I remember being extremely careful about my appearance around Lorraine, lest she make some comment (to someone else, not me!) if I didn't pass inspection.

Several years passed, and Lorraine decided to attend a weight loss program and successfully lost thirty pounds. One day I stopped by her house only to observe that she was wearing slacks. I couldn't resist the urge to comment on that fact. Her response:

"Oh, I only said that because I didn't look good in them myself." Her insecurity drove her rudeness to dangerous levels. Lorraine's lack of self-confidence wounded so many hearts; if only she'd worked as hard relying on God for her sense of worth as she did on slashing and maiming those she perceived as a threat.

Insecurity is often what causes anger; we don't like something about ourselves and go on the offensive. We assume everyone is thinking what we already know about ourselves. However, we can say something negative about ourselves but no one else is allowed. But we will deny with our last breath that we're wounded and angry. Good Christians don't exhibit those emotions.

That is what makes us so dangerous to ourselves and others; we pretend that we aren't angry. Practice that behavior long enough and we might even have ourselves convinced. Then we wonder why our relationships are shaky and we are suspicious about what we see and hear.

Husbands are often caught in the rudeness trap. If a man tells his wife she looks nice today, she wants to know why he thought she looked bad the day before. If he compliments her dinner preparations, his dear wife accuses him of hating all her other meals.

A professor once asked our graduate level counseling class for an example of a double bind, which is commonly referred to as a no-win situation. Here was the winning response: "Honey, do I look fat in these jeans?"

Sarcasm

Let me set the record straight, in some instances sarcasm can be downright hilarious! One of my fondest memories of sarcasm done safely was during a family outing to a pizza place. My son Ryan was in grade school and well known for reciting television quotes.

His favorite show at the time was old *Saturday Night Live* episodes—especially when the character Stuart Smalley was featured. Sitting in the quiet restaurant with his grandparents, parents, and sister, Ryan stated, "I'm good enough, I'm smart enough, and doggone it, people like me."

Without blinking an eye, his Grandpa responded with the comment: "Name one."

Due to the perfect timing and expression of the retort, it took us a good five minutes to control our laughter. Because it was safe and because it was truly funny, we all enjoyed it immensely. No one's feelings were sacrificed to get a laugh.

The difference between fun sarcasm and harmful sarcasm is motive—*why* something is said.

I can say, "Man, your feet are so big you can stomp grapes" and because I'm in a trusting relationship with a friend or family member it can be funny...especially if the recipient of the comment knows my heart (and so do I).

But if I make the same comment, "Man, your feet are so big you can stomp grapes" when I want to be a jerk, it takes on a whole new meaning:

a) You're gargantuan.

b) I think you're a freak.

c) You're a loser.

One comment involves rudeness because of the motive, yet the other does not because it is just me being goofy. See the difference?

Like most newly married couples, my husband and I had little expendable income. Yet much of our leisure time was spent window shopping, dreaming of "someday."

Don began teasing me that I could sniff out a mall in a strange town within minutes. Perhaps some relationships use such comments to hurl hidden barbs and insults at each other; Don meant it as a matter of pride that my retail sniffer was so highly tuned! I knew his heart and felt safe, even if at times his sarcasm was obvious.

Don't Raise Your Eyebrows So Loud!

Rudeness is also expressed in nonverbal behaviors. Books are written on how to read body language and the hidden messages behind a shrug or a sigh. Folded arms, loss of eye contact, and closed-off stances indicate a bad attitude in the making.

Early in my career I began meeting with a husband and wife for marriage counseling. Their casual demeanor at our first session belied the anger they felt toward each other.

After asking them about why they'd come for professional help, I had to sit back in amazement. I felt like I was sitting ringside at a boxing match as each individual competed to get my attention and convince me that their grievances were greater than the other's woes. Their behavior was so uncontrollable I could only observe during that first session. The next time we met I began by establishing rules and boundaries:

"You may not grunt, gasp, sigh, or whimper if you don't like what is being said. You may not mutter under your breath while the other person is talking. You may not roll your eyes, stomp your feet, or shift in your chairs as if in pain. You may not make rude gestures or insult each other in my presence. Do you have any questions?"

This husband and wife looked at each other, looked back at me, and then, as if by some prearranged signal, began waving their hands to get called on like they were in elementary school! If it weren't so blatantly disrespectful I'd have laughed out loud.

During their treatment, I was forced to keep a coach whistle in my desk drawer and would use it several times a session.

This is an exaggerated example of rudeness (albeit a true one). It is a method whereby we send signals to others that we don't approve of or appreciate what is being said or done. And it is extremely effective.

My husband Don and I have now been married over twenty-five years and it's almost funny how a couple learns to communicate without words:

[I look at him]

[He raises his eyebrows inquiringly]

[I look away, shaking my head]

[He shifts his weight in his chair, sighing deeply]

[I look back at him, my eyes squinting suspiciously]

[He rolls his eyes, looks away and tosses his magazine on the floor]

[I stand up and stomp out of the room]

We just had an argument and no one said a single word! That's how we experience rudeness—we communicate displeasure behind a mask of innocence. Our body language says everything so we can deny our intentions and make the other person appear wrong.

God Knows Our Thoughts

The point I'm making here is that we may fool ourselves and others about our behavior, but we'll never fool God. He knows our hearts and motives and He wants us to be willing to discern them as well.

Just recently I found myself explaining this concept to a couple during a counseling session. During our discussion, I observed several of their rude behaviors and brought them to their attention.

Ramone admitted that when he touched Gina's knee

before he shared something potentially unflattering about her, he was silently putting up a barrier to forestall her anger. Then, when Gina responded in a joking but sarcastic tone, she saw that she was also being rude to protect herself emotionally.

Neither one of these people was overtly trying to be hurtful. However, those covert actions are noticed by the Holy Spirit dwelling within each of us and they remain stuck in our memory. Then the low grade irritation begins and builds as we experience these actions on a continuous basis. No wonder our tempers get triggered and we lose our self-control, wondering afterwards what exactly it was that started it all.

When you gain confidence from each success with LSMU, you will feel safe as God makes you aware of your own thoughts and behaviors before you express them. Even as you experience the situation, you can become aware of how your words sound and then take responsibility for the motives behind them.

Rudeness Toward Yourself

This brings us to the most prevalent use of rudeness; that which we heap on ourselves. Self deprecating humor is one thing; I find it refreshing to find someone able to not take herself too seriously (you know who you are!). Having the ability to "get the joke" and enjoy laughing with others can really unite people.

One year, Don and I went with my parents and brothers on a cruise. Every meal…and there were legions…I would say I wanted every dessert. There was no hidden agenda in my statements because I really *did* want every dessert!

It finally came to the last evening of the last day of the trip. At dinner that night I was distracted by the attention of at least five waiters, each carrying several desserts which they grandly arranged in front of me.

Unbeknownst to me, someone at my table had asked the head waiter to bring me one of each dessert they had on the menu. So here I sat with all those goodies; in fact, my companions had to move down the table to make room for them all (Say, is this Heaven?).

I had a choice: I could get angry because "someone" was making fun of me, or I could go along with the fun, pass out extra forks, and get to eating. Guess which one I picked. And it turned into a fun memory we all still laugh about.

This is Different

But there is the rudeness that we express toward ourselves in our everyday lives. The negative comments we make about ourselves aimed at our weaknesses and flaws. We editorialize about our height, weight, body parts, clothing choices, and so on, to indicate a lack of acceptance and underlying anger toward who we are intrinsically. We roll our eyes when we can't find our car keys, and mutter under our breath when we overlook an appointment. It's as if we think, "You don't have to tell me I'm imperfect; I'll tell *you* I'm imperfect and give examples."

How many times have we made unflattering comments about our wrinkles, gray hair, or extra pounds? How about using sarcasm to describe how you need a crane to help you get out of a chair? I could go on and on because I hear these comments almost every day. And I make these comments myself.

My Nightmare Begins

Many years ago I attended a three-day ladies' retreat in Chicago with a group of friends from church. I was just emerging from a painful church-related trauma and was tentatively stepping out again by attending this Christian gathering.

It was restful and encouraging until the second day. A friend (Donna) and I had gone back to the hotel room to change for lunch, rushing so we could meet up with other ladies from our group. We made pretty good time until I discovered that I couldn't find my other shoe. As I searched for it I became frustrated, worried that I was delaying our groups' lunch plans (I had learned from experience that you just don't get in the way of a female and her food!).

Hoping to indicate that I didn't want to be a problem, I made some disparaging comment about myself because I couldn't find my shoe. Before I knew it Donna had stopped dead in her tracks.

"That's it. I've had enough. I want you to say three good things about yourself."

I thought she was bluffing and said so. She was unmoved.

"I have heard you say bad things about yourself for too long. I'm not moving until you say three good things about yourself."

By this time several other ladies from our group had come looking for us (remember what I said about the food?). I tried to use them as an excuse, "Can't keep them waiting," but she still refused to budge. By this time sweat was trickling down the small of my back as I realized I was cornered—with witnesses.

I tried to brush Donna off by saying "I like the color blue," but she wasn't having it. She said, "I want to hear about who you really are and I have to agree."

Why wasn't the earth opening up to swallow me whole? I was certainly praying for that to happen.

More ladies were coming in search of us; by now there were about six women standing around me waiting for an answer. The sweat was really flowing now.

"Um...I'm a loyal friend."

Donna agreed and so did the other ladies.

"I'm creative."

So far so good.

"And um...I'm a sincere mom."

That seemed to appease the masses and so we began to exit the room. I was so relieved I said, "Man, I'm glad that's over. I don't think I'm smart enough to come up with anymore."

The crowd stopped and turned to me en masse. Donna, who had initiated this whole ordeal in the first place, glared at me and said, "I want you to say three good things about yourself."

Zapped!

By the time the weekend was over I'd been zapped thirteen times! After awhile I found myself trying to come up with answers ahead of time just in case I got caught again.

This experience made me realize how very rude I tended to be toward myself. My heart longed for acceptance, yet here I was making statements about my imperfections that proved that I hadn't even accepted myself. Negative opinions were so much a part of my identity that I was ineffectual in many areas of my life. I mean, someone as flawed as me can't be used by God, right?

Once when teaching LSMU to a group of ladies, I brought up the rudeness issue. It really struck a nerve that night as each woman seemed to identify with my personal observations. A seemingly confident woman loudly disagreed with me, however, as she explained that making comments like that serves to make other people feel more comfortable. Trying to explain my position, I said, "That's like having someone break into your house intent on murder. You're saying you would rush into the kitchen and begin stabbing yourself with a butcher knife so the potential attacker feels more comfortable."

And that's what we do. We are the first to ridicule ourselves and disguise it behind jokes and sarcasm. Yet, when we're alone we admit that we're angry that we have flaws bad enough that we have to mock our very identities. Ultimately, we're telling God that He messed up in how He put us together.

Lessons Learned the Hard Way

There was something else I learned about myself that weekend in Chicago. After spending so much time searching for positive aspects of my life, I realized that I wasn't as useless as I thought I was. When you think about it, I was able to come up with thirty-nine positive traits and none of them were duplicates. On top of that, an entire group of women agreed with my statements, so they must have seen value in me that I was unable or unwilling to see on my own. I realized that I'd been selling myself short in my own eyes and, in doing so, insulting the God who created me.

Let me share a true example of how "feigned ignorance" can affect those we love the most. We often think we're alone in our little worlds and that everyone else is unaware and therefore unaffected by our thoughts and feelings. Nothing could be further from the truth!

From the time Don and I began dating, I'd get into discouraged funks and make negative comments about myself: "I'm fat, I'm ugly, I'm stupid." Time after time, Don would go to great lengths to assure me that these opinions were not true. He would assure me that he felt I was wonderful and beautiful, etc., etc., etc. But I wouldn't believe him. I'd accuse him of ulterior motives, certain that he had an agenda and couldn't truly believe what he was trying to make me believe.

Finally, one evening it all came to a boiling point. By now we'd been together for more than ten years, meaning that for most of that time Don had been forced to endure endless nights of listening to me either cry myself to sleep or complain about myself.

I'd been going through my nightly tirade (I could recite it in my sleep) regarding my imperfections. But this time Don had enough of being the strong silent type; he lost it.

He bolted upright in bed and began pounding his fists on the mattress yelling, "Can't you see what you're *doing*? Every time you criticize yourself you are insulting *me*! I'm your husband! I chose you; I prayed that God would give me a godly wife! I prayed for you. When you complain about yourself you are saying that I have *bad taste*!! What do you think that says about *me*?!"

I sat there in stunned silence. I was shocked by Don's reaction to what was so normal for me. But I was also humbled when I discovered that I had never once thought of my negative attitude in that perspective. I finally realized that every time I said something unflattering about myself, I was hurting those who loved me; after all, they chose me. My viewpoint had always been all about me and my flaws; I never once considered the effect that viewpoint would have on my dear friends and family members.

I took it one step further; God chose me, He created me. When I griped and groaned about my multitude of flaws, what I was essentially claiming was that God made a mistake! No matter what Scripture proclaims is absolutely true and lovely, I had refused to believe it.

Continuing this concept brings us to a frightening conclusion:

If I'm refuting a statement uttered by God, my Creator, my Protector, my Guide...then what I'm really doing is saying that *God is wrong* and *I am right*. My effort to appear humble and self-effacing is, instead, a stand-off between me and the One who created the very air I breathe!

As you read the above paragraph, honestly examine your own attitude about your apparent lack of positive attributes and force yourself to be real for a moment. Is your anger regarding your flaws due to your preferences—meaning, being petite but wishing you were tall, brunette wanting to be blonde, curly hair vs. straight hair? It's an ironic fact that no matter what gifts are present, there is always a desire to have something else.

In my own case, I always thought that being an extroverted optimist was a major flaw. I longed to be the wallflower at a gathering so I could disappear if I said something wrong or inappropriate (which I often thought was every time I said anything!). I learned later that the introverts were longing to be like *me*, wishing they could at least think of something to say in a social situation. How funny that we grab onto the belief that our talents and attributes are a fluke, while everyone else is thought to have more of an "in" with God. The ongoing argument we have with God is that it seems as if He put more time into the talents He's given to everyone else than He has put into us.

It's No Fun if You Have to Work at It!

Before we move away from this topic, let me share a huge lesson I've learned the hard way. Hopefully you'll understand it much faster than I did, thereby allowing you more peaceful sleep and less agony in the long run.

The fact is, we're all given certain talents and gifts. Scripture talks about how each of us is a distinctive part of the body of Christ, and we are all given certain gifts we are to use for His glory (Romans 12:4–6).

But what I've noticed is that we seem to only place value on *other* people's talents rather than our own. For instance, I've often envied (yes, envied) those who can sing before large groups of people and hardly break a sweat. Both of my children are musical and it excites them to be able to perform before an audience. Me, I pray for the rapture to come…*now*! I can't perform that gift with joy. I also have envied those who can organize, delegate, and lead a major event to its positive conclusion. On the other hand, it's a great success for me if I remember to show up….

I remember when the Lord gave me release from those yearnings. I was sitting in church, once more envying a performer who was making it look so effortless to play an instrument and sing along with the melody. The thought occurred to me, "Karen, if we could all do that, it wouldn't be a gift."

My head jerked up and my eyes widened as if I'd been jolted with a cattle prod.

It was true! If everyone could demonstrate the same abilities it wouldn't be considered special, nor would it be as great a blessing.

Over the years I've counseled individuals who have grieved over perceived failings as they express a wish that they could do or be something else. As they share their flaws, they also share their interests. Before too long they begin to understand that the gifts that God has given them have been overlooked because they were deemed too easy. I mean, would we call it a gift if we had to move mountains to use it? Extroverted performers need introverted organizers to make sure they know where to go and when to show up; behind the scenes doers need someone or something to do *for*.

So when we admit anger toward God, as it pertains to our definition of valuable opposed to His, who is ultimately in charge of your life?

Who's going to win?

That's Not Rudeness, It's Humility!

Most of us have difficulty accepting compliments. We are raised to believe that we should *give* praise to someone, but we shouldn't *accept* it. I always thought that to accept a compliment was to be boastful and conceited, "Why yes, I look fabulous, I'm so glad you noticed it too." But during my research of rudeness, the Holy Spirit reminded me of how I felt when I praised someone who was unable to accept the compliment. I would then feel really stupid, compelled to prove my sincerity. It wasn't too long before I realized that when my compliments weren't being accepted graciously, I was in essence being told that I had bad taste!

"I really like your blouse."

"What *this* old thing? It doesn't fit me right and is the wrong color. I should just throw it away."

Without meaning to, this individual just told me that I like ugly old shirts I'd probably have to rescue from a dumpster! The response certainly does nothing to endear me to that person nor does it encourage confidence in my own opinions.

We really do depend greatly on what other people think. Somehow we surrender our faith in ourselves and defer to the opinion of others. Several years ago, I personally noted how most of my house was decorated the same way a dear friend whose taste I admired had her own house adorned. I had convinced myself that I couldn't make any decorating decisions without her approval. Over time, I systematically gave up every vestige of personal confidence that I had the ability to create an attractive home and laid the entire burden for decision making at her feet.

Phyllis, a client I'd been seeing for at least a year, often lamented that her appearance was lacking and she was sure that other people were most likely criticizing her privately for her lack of taste.

As I attempted to bring about a new perspective I said, "Did you know I'm color blind?"

"No."

"Yes, I'm blue/green color blind, so what you see as blue I see as a sickly brown."

"Really?"

"So when you ask me if I like your blue shirt I have to say no, because my eyes tell me the color is weird. Does that mean it's really an ugly color?"

"No."

"So why would you measure your worth by how I see color?"

"But..."

"But nothing. Because of the way I see things, you are kicking yourself and judging yourself to be bad. And it's merely a matter of ability and perspective. See what I mean?"

Two of the most difficult words to say as a Christian woman are: "thank you."

To utter these words means I choose to overlook years of hearing that I am unworthy and I must be humble. It means I'm going to accept the opinion of someone else and that I will not squirm under the attention the compliment attracts.

"And You Thought That Would Work?"

Hang with me awhile and you will become aware that I love irony. I think God does too; why else would He state in I Corinthians 1:26–29 that "the foolish shall confound the wise, the weak shall confound the mighty"? I especially love to laugh at our consternation when we get exactly what we asked God for in our prayers. We plead and beg God to change us, to make us into servants of His, and to create a vessel worthy of Him. Then when the changing begins, and the growing pains start, we whine and moan and kick against the molding process.

The same concept is true when we consider our attitudes about compliments. We purchase clothing to make us attractive, wear makeup to enhance our beauty, exercise to enable us to be healthy and fit, yet when our hard work gets noticed we push it away as if it were smelly old gym socks. This is another example of how confusing we can be to our friends and family. If they don't say anything they get in trouble, but if they *do* compliment us they get brushed aside with, "You *have* to say that, you're my husband (mother, sister, uncle, best friend, etc…)."

If we ever need proof that God is long-suffering and patient, this is it! As we grumble, beg, and bargain with God, it is truly amazing that we don't hear His mighty voice rumble, "AAARRRGGGHH! MAKE UP YOUR MIND!!!"

So, repeat these words after me:
"Thank you."
That was feeble. Try again.
"Thank you."
Better, but still weak.
"Thank you."
With some practice you will improve. It is true that these are only two words in our entire vocabulary. Yet

these words will pave the way for more trusting relationships and thus can be the catalyst to break down the habitual wall of rudeness that often defeats genuine communication.

So I suggest you force yourself to master the "thank you" concept; no editorializing, no dissertation is necessary. You don't even have to agree with the comments. LSMU will enable you to keep your opinions to yourself until you have time to think and pray about them. The goal is to not cause damage (or be damaged) in the meantime.

Let me challenge you when you are tempted to be critical of yourself or others. Spend time thinking of your true motives when you respond sarcastically or with manipulative, angry behaviors. Then let God lead you to willingly accept and move past this angry display as He reveals your value as His child.

So Now What?

So now it's time to "get to getting" and learn the skills necessary to overcome the maladaptive cycle of behavior that got us into this mess. I've been transparent and shared my own issues with you; now it's your turn to take these tools and allow your hands and mind to get accustomed to using them.

Here's where we come to a crossroad. Most of us are wired so we fit into one of two categories:

"Yeah, but…"

or

"What if?"

A "yeah, but"' personality will eagerly read this information then sit back with lots of examples explaining why it won't work.

"Yeah, but she doesn't know *my* family."

"Yeah, but she hasn't had *my* trauma."

"Yeah, but my circumstances make it impossible to keep from losing my temper"

(kindly refer to the chapter on pride if this is your position...).

This person will quote chapter and verse, citing situations where he or she was the innocent party and was sideswiped anyway. The viewpoint is one of solitary suffering; no one in the entire world has ever been treated as unfairly as she has (Ummmm.....ever read the book of Job?).

The "what if" personality willingly hears the information, but then seeks ways to close down any possible loophole that could ever possibly arise in the formula.

"Okay, what if I do all these things and let God have my worries and go home tonight and nothing turns out the way I want them to? What if I do all this changing and God doesn't come through for me? What if in twelve years my daughter gets married and has trouble in her marriage because I didn't learn this early enough to help her in her life?"

Come on, I know you've heard people say these things, and I know you've said them because I've heard you! Of all the comments, suggestions, or snide remarks I've heard, this one tops them all:

"Yeah, but...what if it doesn't work?"

If that's your concern, it's important that you remind yourself of God's promises. Read through this next chapter, try it, and *then* make your decision.

By the way, I know that statement has been made because I heard it with my own ears...uttered from my own lips...

Six

Lord, Shut Me Up!

"Watch Out Temper, Here I Come!"

LSMU has become a catch phrase among my clients and group attendees who have embraced its value in their lives, and now I offer it to you. It is a means by which you can regain personal control by relying on God for help in times of great stress and conflict. It is intended for both internal and external pressures. Often we find that we are our own worst enemy as we convince ourselves we can handle just one more hassle before we snap. Such is not the case since one of the first abilities we lose during conflict is our sense of discernment.

Not Patience Again!

So here goes. Remember that patience is seeking the truth from God. The truth is not a popularity contest that one must win in order to be right. It is also not a debate that creates a controversy that must be argued pro or con. The truth is what is accurately being depicted in a situation and has no winners or losers.

The idea of LSMU is to use patience for the purpose for which it is intended; it is meant to allow time to examine the conflict and do internal fact finding before coming to a decision about it. Patience is something to willingly choose, rather than being cornered in an apparently hopeless situation and used as a last resort.

Think about the last time you were driving in an unfamiliar town. You thought you knew the driving directions, but after several U-turns it became apparent that you were hopelessly lost. Did you start yanking on the steering wheel as you veered crazily across five lanes of traffic, waiting for a magic sign to appear telling you which direction to drive? Or did you pull onto the side of the road, pull out a map, and calmly attempt to get your bearings?

LSMU is to serve as your map. Your responsibility is to calm down and get your bearings before you head out on the road.

"Is It Hot in Here Or Is It Just Me?"

Most, if not all of us, experience a physical reaction to conflict. I feel heat in my chest or face; some individuals report clenched teeth, breaking a sweat, feeling prickly, or out of breath. Whatever the physical symptom, it is a signal that you are negatively responding to something.

The very fact that you're experiencing physical symptoms indicates that something is amiss at this point. Whenever you feel frightened, hopeless, hurt, or confused in your relationship with God, or with someone else, this means that there's an emotional response to the situation. The trick is to keep these feelings from controlling your thoughts and actions.

You don't need to understand the "whys" and the "who did what to whom" at this point. This is the time to respect the Holy Spirit speaking to your heart and mind and to respond by saying:

"Lord, shut me up!"

Notice that the request is *not* "Lord, shut me down." This is not an effort on your part to rationalize why you shouldn't have this emotional/physical response. I am not working to ignore the perceived conflict, nor am I suggesting you immediately take the underdog position during a disagreement and pretend it isn't happening.

What is important is that you demonstrate your willingness to step aside emotionally to gather facts about the situation. Stop talking and arguing about it with the other person (or God, or even yourself), and excuse yourself mentally or physically, *for the purpose of taking time to think and pray.*

This is often where other anger management programs stop. If a person can control themselves during an incident, it's considered a success. But if the fact-finding isn't followed up with thought and prayer, where does the pent up anger go?

Well, I'll tell you! When we merely ignore the situation and do nothing to resolve it, we are storing that information deep within our hearts until it bubbles up unexpectedly—usually at the worst possible time (like getting the giggles in church).

Wheeeeeee!

Picture if you will a waterslide at a fun park. When my children were younger we visited water parks because it was something we all enjoyed. I would even willingly wriggle into a swimsuit for the occasion. It was so much fun to climb up all those steps until we would reach the platform at the very top.

Once there, an impossibly bronzed helper would instruct us on how to position ourselves in the chute so we could obtain the best and safest ride possible. I would always remark how long the trudge up the stairs took in relation to the extremely short ride back down.

When the way was clear, we would each push off in turn and be at the mercy of the twists and turns of the ride until we would ultimately plop into the pool at the end.

Not very gracefully, I might add.

One thing I noticed, however, was that once I committed to taking the ride I was totally at its mercy—there was no way I could turn back even if I wanted to. The same is true when we decide to ignore the warning signals that let us know we're about to lose control. To feel the sweaty palms or tightening facial muscles and not heed them is the same as pushing off the waterslide; you are at the mercy of something that will carry you off until you land unceremoniously at the bottom. Once there, you experience two emotions: relief that the ride is over and you survived, and remorse due to the damage you now must attempt to repair.

Get Me My Rubber Room!

I've even gone so far as to describe the experience of going down the waterslide as a type of temporary insanity, because once you push off there is no way you can listen to reason. You couldn't stop the momentum even if you wanted to. Now really, have you ever seen anyone at a water park stop in the middle of the ride? Or have you had the ability to dig in and say, "I changed my mind"? The very nature of the ride is to experience the force of gravity to its very end.

That is exactly how it feels in the midst of an anger surge; there is an uncontrollable power that has us in its grasp until every last word is uttered no matter how unpleasant. During the verbal attack, many folks have reported a sense within themselves that said, "What are you *doing*?" and they still can't stop the behavior. Why? Because they're at the mercy of the waterslide.

To be able to say "Lord, shut me up!" at the first sense of danger is to take responsibility for the outcome. It's to acknowledge a problem without needing an explanation; the very act of LSMU is to mentally take a step back from the platform and take a breather. We often even sense a lessening of the internal tension associated with the conflict since we are stepping out of line for the reckless ride. Consider it the second wind needed to finish a difficult task. You retain the energy to maintain emotional control of your anger.

The idea here is to interrupt the momentum that is building during the conflict itself. If there is an accelerating argument, someone has to have the strength to extinguish the progress; no fuel, no fire. If you refuse to respond as you usually do, you will disrupt the cycle and it will have nowhere to go. That is not to say you are to shut down or no longer have an opinion. It simply means you are choosing to sit back and sift through the facts rather than wade through ugly emotions.

Just Where Do You Think You're Going?

There are certain circumstances that can prevent someone from excusing themselves physically during a conflict. Specifically, it is not a good idea to try to leave a vehicle speeding down a busy highway (don't laugh—several clients complained that their spouses wouldn't let them jump out of the car! Their reasoning was that they were trying to excuse themselves from the conflict).

Also, I personally wouldn't want my neurosurgeon to walk out of the operating room in a snit if he became irritated with his nursing staff. Call me selfish ...

Finally, you must discern whether it is wiser for you to remain in the room so that you show respect to the other person or to walk out simply because you can. I've been asked many times if I thought it was better to stay or go. My response is, "How would *you* feel if someone walked out on you during an argument?" The point is that personal safety is an entirely different matter than personal responsibility. Only you will know at that time if it's better to stay or go. Just keep in mind that you can't do much fact finding if you're in another room.

There is a purpose behind patience and it isn't simply to avoid conflict. In fact, I'm not suggesting we avoid conflict at all. Jesus didn't and we aren't supposed to either. But let's face it; Jesus used patience even when he became angry. After all, Peter was the disciple who was continually taking those out-of-control waterslide rides and they weren't even invented yet!

What I urge you to do is step away from the slide for the purpose of taking time to think about what you have just seen and heard, and to pray for wisdom about it. Seek the facts and discuss them with God as you pray about the situation and look for His will in what you should do next.

"Now THAT'S Gonna Cost You"

I never thought about moving beyond the current crisis to seek God's leading when I personally defined patience. I always felt patience was merely survival in the face of trials. Take the beating and be quiet.

Then, if I did manage to endure, I would grit my teeth and tell God He owed me one.

But LSMU focuses on patience being the deliberate choice to stay in the difficulty to gather information needed to present the true issue before God. And that's what makes the difference.

Step One: "Lord, shut me up!"

Pray for insight about yourself. "Am I being a jerk? Did I have a bad day?" Hold your tongue (don't say anything you might have to apologize for later). Don't make assumptions (he/she did that on purpose), draw conclusions (here it goes again, just like always; it'll never change), or take any physical action at this point (no vase throwing, wedding ring tossing, and *please* don't try to jump out of a speeding minivan!).

Step Two: "Help me hear You."

Your goal is to maintain a level of submission before God and willingness to learn so that you can gather the facts intelligently. Many of us shut down during a conflict as a self-defense mechanism. We use "limo windows" (the glass wall that separates the driver from those who are seated in the back of the limousine) to stay in the situation, but hear nothing. Imagine mentally activating the mute button on the TV remote. You can see the picture just fine, but there is no sound (many of us think our families use this technique on us even when we're *not* in conflict!). Seeking grace from God will give you the ability to submit your mind, will, and emotions to Him *in this situation*.

It is important to note the words *in this situation* because you must remember to keep each conflict separate from any other. We usually get these grand notions that we're never going to lose our tempers again, we're never going to say or do the wrong thing once we learn this process of patience.

Well, think again. No sooner do you make that vow than you break it. It would be like resolving to never have another piece of chocolate. Once you break that resolution (and you will) your sense of failure could cause you to give up entirely, convinced that this LSMU thing may work for other people, but not for you. But if you remind yourself that it is your choice to submit to God for this occurrence only, your chances of success will greatly increase.

Also, to *state in this situation* is to remind ourselves not to throw in old arguments along with the current one. Many times we call attention to something that happened last week, last year, or even ten years ago. Then the battle becomes a matter of who has the longest memory and/or who can hold the biggest grudge. *In this situation* becomes a personal promise to keep the argument current and not to dilute the matter with old issues. It can be difficult at first, but the value of adhering to this decision will make the conflict easier to settle.

One more thing: the majority of the conflicts we encounter are actually very brief in duration. What seems like an eternity in real time is in reality often less than fifteen to twenty minutes. Most are even briefer.

What makes the discomfort last so long is the simmering and reviewing and reacting to what just took place. I've had clients check their clocks after a fight; almost all of them noted in shock that the interaction lasted less than five to ten minutes.

So when I say *in this situation* I'm not even suggesting you sacrifice days or weeks of your life (I would be if I was asking you to hold your breath, but that's different). I'm proposing that when you pray LSMU *in this situation* it is truly a doable task.

When we say LSMU we are referring to not only external frustrations that cause us to lose our cool and say the first thing that comes to our minds. It also applies to a list of internal thoughts that are inaccurate and lead to obsessive opinions and ideas. Internal thoughts such as:

"I'm so stupid."

"I'm fat."

"I'm ugly."

"No one could really love someone like me."

"I said that wrong."

"I did this wrong."

"I should have known better."

LSMU is a useful aid in preventing the self-defeating behaviors that cause anxiety and can have a negative influence on our relationships. Many individuals report that they use LSMU more for confirming their own identity in Christ than in conflict with other people.

Imagine once more the sensation of traveling down a waterslide at an amusement park. The general consensus is that one's senses are compromised during the descent; I for one can't hear anything except for the sound of water flying past my ears and my own voice as I scream the whole way down! I am unable to hear anything else. So in a conflict when I am blinded by my own anger and physical response, I cannot hear the Holy Spirit telling me to be calm. Nor are you if you were to be honest about it. When we are able to pray LSMU at the first sign of tension, we are stepping back and retaining our ability to hear and reason.

SHHH! It's a Secret!

There is one warning I'd like to offer, however. Consider this a little tip that could save you lots of nights on the living room sofa. Or a week at your mom's. Or a tent in the back yard...

When you are in conflict and feel the physical reaction in your body, remember that LSMU is an internal request and not a verbal one. To state, "Lord, Shut Me Up!" when you're toe to toe with someone is the same as looking heavenward and yelling, "God, give me strength!" It's a guaranteed way to worsen the situation as you proclaim your martyrdom to the rafters. LSMU is an internal prayer request between you and God.

Keep it silent and private.

After the Conflict

Step #3: "Here are my facts"

The next step in LSMU occurs some time after the situation has passed; ideally on the same day if time permits. This is when the heat of the battle has dissipated and life has continued its normal routine. Again, here is where many of us make our first mistake; we believe that since the conflict is over we are supposed to move on as if nothing had happened.

NO NO NO!

This is the most crucial portion of biblical anger management. It is taking the time to stop, think, and seek God's perspective regarding what you've just seen and heard and experienced. Turn it over to the Holy Spirit as you focus on (not obsess over) the experience. No, we don't turn the other cheek just yet. Nor do we "forget those things which are behind" (Phil. 3:14). Not until we've methodically analyzed each step in LSMU.

I explain Step 3 like this:

Once there is a lull in the activities of the day, find a quiet spot and allow yourself to calm your heart and mind. Then begin the process of prayer:

"Here are my facts, Lord. Mr. Smith came into my office today and told me that I'm the worst counselor he has ever seen."

No editorializing, no adding or subtracting from the statement. State the literal facts to God *as you see them* concerning *only this situation.* Report it as if you were sending an old-time telegram and had to pay per word. Keep it brief.

Step 4: "Here are my feelings"

This is where you have the freedom to share your thoughts and feelings about the situation:

"What Mr. Smith said made me feel irritated, insulted, disrespected, and angry. I think he's a jerk, Lord. Who does he think he is? I think he was mean and selfish. I don't feel as if I deserved to be spoken to like that...." And so on.

See what I'm getting to? The point is that you are purposefully stopping to acknowledge before God what you really thought and felt during and about the altercation. Remember, you don't have to have documentation to prove that you are right about what you saw; in fact, you don't *have* to be right. It's your perception and that's what we're focusing on. No excuses are allowed for or against the situation. This is an example of a woman's tendency to rationalize when someone is being a jerk to her:

"When Mr. Smith told me I'm a terrible counselor I felt upset, but I understand that he has lots of stress in his life and that he's scared and looking for someone to blame." When we rationalize, we are subconsciously saying that our perceptions and feelings don't count, which is untrue.

So say what you think and don't make excuses for anyone or anything. God already knows how we feel and is waiting for us to be real and admit it.

I call it my opportunity to have a spiritual temper tantrum. You are relying on the fact that God will reveal the truth to you in due time. But right now you are honestly stating your grievances to Him and not inflicting them on anyone else. Don't be reluctant to fully express every facet of your dissatisfaction about the conflict with God....He can take it!

"You'll Never Believe What So and So Said..."

How often do we have a run-in with someone and can't wait to share it with folks who aren't even involved? I've even had friends call me on the phone *during* a fight to tell me about it! The value of only sharing it with God is that once the disagreement is over we don't have to try to do damage control with everyone we've involved along the way. Many people prejudice their families and friends toward someone by griping about them in a fit of anger. That is unfair and causes long term hard feelings that are difficult to heal.

I have been guilty of this behavior myself; although it's satisfying to know that your friends and/or family cares enough about you to want to protect you, it's uncomfortable to explain should you and the "transgressor" settle your differences. So I caution you to keep these grievances private until the Holy Spirit reveals the truth to you.

Step 4 is only for our benefit since God already knows how we feel about the situation and the individual causing it. In reality, we need to dig in and fully admit our thoughts and feelings about this no matter how unflattering it may be to us personally. It is imperative that we take advantage of the freedom to admit our anger and allow our flaws to be examined by God. Using honesty and humility is the only way we can communicate with God and expect an answer (Psalm 66:18).

After we fully acknowledge the facts and our feelings about this situation we can then progress to resolution. Resolution can come immediately, or it can sometimes take several hours or even several days as we wait on God for the answer to the situation.

It goes like this:

Step 5: "Am I Right?"

Did I see the situation right? Was I correct or justified in my perception of the problem? Was this conflict accurately perceived and appropriately acted upon?

Ask God to give you an awareness of your current attitude about this problem or person:

"Am I being Christ-like? Was I really as innocent in this conflict as I'd like to think I was? Did Mr. Smith (or Leonard, or Ozzie…) come out of nowhere and attack me for no reason? Was I completely right here?"

Step 6: "Am I Wrong?"

Did I enter the interaction with a bad attitude? Was I tired or hungry or coming down with the flu; was I looking for a reason to be rude and ill-tempered? Was I irritated by an old argument that was left unsettled and saw this disagreement as an excuse to pick up where that one left off?"

Often I'm still in the middle of this process when I realize I was the instigator of the conflict. Most of my overreactions are caused by my perception that I'm being disrespected or mistreated; they can be continuations of something that frustrated me earlier in the day that was left unresolved. In essence, I'm looking for a fight. I'm stalking my prey, just watching and waiting for someone to get in my cross hairs. When they do, I pour out my angst and frustrations until I've dumped it all on them.

Most of us with anger issues have the same attitude. We trip and stub our toe, can't find our car keys, are late to work, miss a deadline, and suddenly we're looking for someone to blame (because our bad day *can't* be because we weren't looking where we were walking, didn't put the keys on the table yesterday, didn't set the alarm clock, or use our time wisely when attempting to get our work done...).

When we exercise our ability to admit before God that we were wrong when we lost our temper, we gain peace knowing that in using LSMU we didn't verbalize it and drag anyone else down with us. It's a comfort to know that it can be corrected simply by acknowledging before God that our attitude in this situation was out of whack.

Notice with care what is being stated here: admitting our crankiness and rash behavior to ourselves and to God is *not* saying that these thoughts and feelings indicate that we as individuals are stupid and worthless. Indeed, the confession is that *what we thought* was askew.

This is the beauty of private confession and repentance. No one else need ever know you struggled with these thoughts and feelings. In comparison, think of the damage control that is necessary if you lose your composure and verbally attack everyone within earshot. No apology ever feels adequate and the regret and self-condemnation is horrible.

If you have ever had a new puppy you will understand this metaphor: Trying to make amends with someone you've emotionally injured is like seeing doggie droppings on the ground and not being able (or willing) to avoid stepping in it: you can clean it off your shoe but the aroma lingers for quite a while afterwards! The value of LSMU is that it enables you to avoid the nasty stuff in the first place (unless you own stock in a poop scooping company....)!

"Would You Like Fries with That?"

When I was still living at home with my parents and siblings, we never said we were sorry after a conflict. We just moped around and sighed a lot until someone would relent. Then, instead of officially apologizing, one of us would ask if the other person would like to share a soda or a sandwich. If he or she said yes, we knew that all was forgiven and we could put the problem behind us.

When we lose control of our anger, we attempt to make it right afterwards, but there is always a residual amount of remorse to contend with. It felt as if all I ever did was make sandwiches! The regret I've felt is grounded in the realization that all the hard work and prayer I've invested in building godly and safe relationships can crumble in an angry instant.

"A wise woman builds her house, but a foolish one plucks it down with her hands." (Proverbs 14:1 NIV)

"He who foams up quickly and flies into a passion deals foolishly, and a man of wicked plots and plans is hated." (Proverbs 14:17 Amp.)

When we are able to back off the waterslide we can maintain a godly sense of self-worth that steadies our emotional footing in relation to who we are in Christ.

As we pursue a workable method in anger management, our minds must be open to be taught the meaning of *Agape* love, which is the spiritual, Christ-like love given by God.

We are to surrender our reliance on our old coping mechanisms such as:

- Our emotions: "He/She makes me so angry!"

- Our fears: "Now I'll be unloved."

- Our assumptions: "He/She did that on purpose to annoy me."

- Our prejudices: "I hate it when someone uses that tone of voice with me."

- Our memories: "My mother/dad/brother/boyfriend/pastor/neighbor used to talk to me like that and I hated it."

- Our willful disobedience: "I want to win no matter what."

You're Asking ME about Normal?

Remember that it sometimes takes time to sort through your thoughts and feelings about the situation; you can't rush it. Submission and obedience to God while you wait for Him to reveal the "am I right or am I wrong" answer means that you must act normally in the meantime. As justified as you feel, you are not to act rude, selfish, angry, or lie in the meantime. This is a tough one! Many of us like to skulk around the house, mope, slam doors, and release deep mournful sighs. Don't do it, as this only adds to the discomfort (especially if God reveals that *you're* the one who is wrong this time!).

"May I Suggest?"

Keep in mind that you aren't the only one who is experiencing a change in reality.

Think of your family and what your sudden (and unexpected self-control) is doing to them. You can expect at least one person to approach you timidly and ask if you're all right. Now, you can't say "yes" even though that's been the predictable answer every other time. We said you couldn't lie!

So here's the answer I suggest to you. I'm illustrating it with the meaning behind each phrase even though it's said all in one sentence:

- "I am feeling a little edgy (You're right in recognizing something's wrong)."

- "But I'm not sure why (It's not necessarily something you've done)."

- "I'm praying about it (I'm taking steps to understand it)."

- "And when I find out what it is, I'll let you know (You won't be left out of the loop)."

"You Mean It Was Me?"

My counseling experience has revealed that about 80 percent of conflicts are due to our own attitudes and interpretations of circumstances. That means that about 20 percent of conflicts are genuinely due to the misconduct of someone else. We will deal with that dilemma in a later chapter. Right now, consider how much of our anger and frustration is likely to be self-inflicted.

You cannot control another person's behavior, but you can control your reaction to that behavior. The steps of LSMU will help you as you learn to accept responsibility for your anger.

You have a choice to allow God to change you!

It won't happen over night, but it will happen if you follow these steps and submit your mind, will, and emotions to God in your daily life.

Hey, Something's Different!

Over time you will notice something very different when you face a conflict; you will observe a sense of safety and even a sense of peace, despite a disagreement. As you successfully defer your emotional responses to the Holy Spirit and wait for His leading, you will see that God has it under control and that you will be safe during the conflict.

Seven

Kindness

Just as most believers have a skewed definition of patience, such is true of kindness. When I thought of kindness I envisioned cookie baking do-gooders who list emptying bedpans as favorite hobbies. I also saw them hosting hospital tours, training therapy animals, and making crafts from used Christmas cards to send to poor children in other countries. These good Samaritans are never inconvenienced, nor do they think anything of leaving their own children waiting at the bus stop on a rainy day so they can deliver care packages to homeless penguins.

Doesn't it seem as if kindness is an attribute for other folks, but not for real live individuals like you and me? I gave up trying to be kind like that years ago because it always seemed phony to me. No one I knew could be consistently nice in that manner, so why attempt it? Besides that, who would respect someone who never said "no" to anyone?

I much preferred to be the outspoken inappropriate black sheep in the family of God. I felt that if I let people know I was capable of acts of kindness they'd have power over me. It was much better, in my opinion, to do kind acts in private so only God and I knew about them. I suspect that these wonderful deeds were being performed only to accrue brownie points in heaven (if God kept track like that I was out of luck anyway).

The true biblical definition of kindness rocked my former notions of the Golden Rule and "turn the other cheek" (Matthew 5:39), (Luke 6:29). Frankly, I wasn't willing to be the quiet self-effacing type. I'm more of a "if I'm going to be wrong, I'll be wrong at the top of my lungs" kinda girl. So the condemnation I always heaped on myself truly hindered my identity in Christ and became a major source of anger in my life. I didn't want to be a goody-two-shoes; I just wanted to be a godly woman.

Nice Isn't Kind!

There is a disparity between the meaning of *kind* and the meaning of *nice*.

The biblical definition of *kind* is to be spiritually useful. Ephesians 4:15a says, "Speak the truth in love." It refers to the concept of being truthful, sometimes painfully honest for the sincere benefit of the other person. "Be ye kind one to another…." (Ephesians 4:32).

At crucial periods of your life when you absolutely need to know the truth about godly decisions and right living, would you ask someone who never gives you a true opinion? Or would you seek out people who have a track record of saying what is right because they care about you and your sense of peace? Many believers shy away from speaking the truth because they fear hurting someone's feelings. These folks may even be afraid of rejection or the loss of a friendship.

Someone who is so concerned about your feelings that they withhold the truth is being…nice. Nice is the epitome of what we Christians are taught a godly person should be. But is that genuine? Helpful? Discerning?

Perhaps another example is in order. When you are honestly seeking the truth about your thoughts and behaviors, wouldn't you seek out someone who is adept at speaking to your heart without destroying your sense of worth? Kindness then is demonstrated by that person loving you enough to tell the truth.

True Confessions

I admit I had a problem with this for many years. It was my understanding that it was godly to say only positive things in front of people, but the truth (*aka* negative opinions) behind their backs! These negative opinions, although not necessarily life shattering, were somehow off limits to the individual involved. It was far easier to whisper to someone sitting beside me in choir that Susie was a terrible housekeeper than it was to offer to help Susie learn cleaning skills. Some time later I realized that I only had close relationships with individuals with whom I shared my true heart, and vice versa.

I also noticed that I lost friends over behaviors of which I was unaware because no one told me about them; it was as if I was supposed to wake up one morning and say, "I upset Mary three months ago when I made a joke about her pet iguana and she didn't appreciate it. That's why she won't return my phone calls."

It really is true that we don't know what we don't know. How many times do we sense a problem with a fellow Christian, a coworker, or a family member and have no idea what it could be? Even if we ask them they often deny it because they're trying to be *nice*.

This situation can be exasperating as we wrack our brains to figure out what happened to change the dynamics of the relationship; the worst part is that had the offended person spoken the truth in love, we could have a specific issue to think and pray about. Then there is potential for reconciliation. But not if there is a lack of kindness wherein nothing is said.

A Victim of "Nice?"

It has been my sad experience to endure a traumatic split from a dearly loved friend and be given no explanation whatsoever as to the reason behind it. The hurt, anger, sense of unreality, and crushing rejection far outweighs any pain I might have felt being told what the offending issues were. As it is, I have been left with a wrenching sense of loss as my imagination runs away with me. To this day, I'm determined to be the kind of spiritually useful friend to others that I want them to be to me.

That is why I am a strong proponent of kindness: if you have a beef with someone, love them enough to tell them so the information can be taken before the Holy Spirit and prayed about privately. Otherwise, they are left holding empty air and wondering what on earth is going on.

In the course of marriage counseling I often hear:

"He should know that made me mad."

"He knows what he said."

"Only a deaf, mute, blind person wouldn't have known that would bother me."

Friend, let me tell you: He probably didn't know! If you're waiting for him to have an epiphany you might as well give up (note Romans 10:14)!

To be truly kind to someone is to love them enough to tell them what they have done, or are doing, to cause problems or injury to you. To wait (we often wimp out by saying we're going to give them another chance) is to set that person up for failure and say "tsk tsk" when they do fail.

Another factor to consider is that if Peggy hurt you by her behavior, she's most likely hurting other people as well. You may endure personal offenses, but if other folks are wounded it's easier to confront Peggy about her actions so that everyone involved can benefit from your truth-telling.

We often cower at the thought of confronting someone about his or her behavior. We fear that in doing so we'll be ridiculed or rejected. We won't be *nice*.

We take so much responsibility for what is said and done that the fear stops us in our tracks; what if we blow it and become a target for the person, or seriously damage our relationship?

Why Oh Why?

The first thing to analyze is your motive. If your motive for the confrontation is to tear down the person (you've got ammunition) and hurt them, then you should refrain from saying anything at this time. That is speaking the truth, perhaps, but not in love. We can probably all give an example of this in our own lives; my mother-in-law Margaret was an excellent example.

I'm not saying that Don's mother, Margaret, wasn't a wonderful person; she successfully raised five strong boys who are all still married. In fact, Don and I were the last ones to wed and it has been over twenty-five years for us. Margaret and Stewart were married over fifty years by the time she passed away in 1998. She was an awesome family matriarch.

But man, watch out when she had you in her sights! She could put you in your place faster than anyone I had ever met before or have met since. When Don and I were newly married she stated, "I love all my daughters-in-law...until they *cross* me." I think I swallowed my tongue that day.

But Margaret used to make such hurtful comments that I would be smashed flat for weeks. Don and I lived in another state and although I loved her, I feared our visits because I never knew what she would say. I would beg Don to stand up for me and protect me from her withering statements. Margaret would comment about how skinny Donnie looked because he was working so hard and then state firmly that I was getting heavy (I wonder what she meant by that?). Finally Don stood up to her one day:

"Mom, it hurts Karen's feelings when you say that stuff to her."

Now get ready because here's where I'm heading as I explain truth without love.

Margaret sat bolt upright as she glared at him and stated, "Well I'm sorry, but she sure looks *fat* to me!"

GULP!

See many people are like Margaret; they believe that it's okay to crush a person as long as they are telling the truth. There is no concern or love involved. That is why we latch onto the old concept of *nice* and try to sweeten our words, often diluting their meaning. Lest we sound judgmental or mean, we say nothing.

I'm not implying that Margaret didn't love me; I'm

positive she did. But she was a steamroller in the name of truth. If what she said hurt you, that was simply too bad.

Kindness = Confrontation

The idea of biblical kindness is to care enough about the person and your relationships that you have the courage to teach and instruct him or her, confronting him or her as necessary. Kindness is being spiritually useful to yourself or someone else so that broken areas can be presented before God. That means kindness/confrontation has nothing to do with us, as the confronter.

It's Not about Me?

I want to emphasize that again: Kindness/confrontation has nothing to do with you as the confronter. It has nothing to do with you and your fears; and has everything to do with the one to whom you are being kind.

Think of your children. When you need to adjust their thinking and behavior, do you put it off because you're afraid they won't like you anymore? Of course not! You love your kids enough to speak the truth so they can learn and grow up to be responsible and contented adults. You wouldn't dream of allowing them to do anything that would bring harm to themselves or anyone else.

So why would it be any different with our adult relationships? Our motives are to teach them so they can learn personal responsibility before God and in their interactions with you and other people.

Being Willing to Confront

Several years ago I found it necessary to confront a Christian co-worker about a long-standing issue. After going through the kindness process (described in the next chapter) she responded by saying she knew it was a problem but didn't want to change. My prior attitude would have been to argue with her to convince her why she needed to submit in this area, but this time was different. That's because I knew I had done what I needed to do and could rest in the knowledge that I had been kind to her. I said, "Listen, what you do with this situation is between you and God. I have done my part; whether or not you act on it is up to you. I am free."

And I meant it.

What someone does with the information you've given them is entirely up to them. You have fulfilled your part of kindness and can have peace knowing you have been obedient to God's leading and can move on without a backward glance.

No fighting, arguing, or convincing. You have just been spiritually useful.

EIGHT

How to Demonstrate Kindness in Conflict

When we discussed patience in Chapter Two, it was stated that about 80 percent of the time our anger is based on our own thoughts, opinions, and judgments. But what do we do with the other 20 percent of the time? What if you go through the steps of LSMU and determine before God that you were faultless in the conflict? Suppose you were simply on the receiving end of someone else's bad day?

Remember that once you go through the LSMU process you will know if the problem originated with you or someone else. Either way, you are responsible for how you react to and reconcile the matter. If you progress through the "am I right?" or "am I wrong?" criteria and discern that you were the offender, you must go before God to confess and repent. Again, the upshot of this process is that the issue is a private one between you and God; you don't have to publish a front page advertisement admitting your involvement or kneel in broken glass to show your repentance.

But if you perceive that at the end of these steps you have been genuinely wronged, you must not allow it to pass by without resolution. Many times as believers we feel that we are to forgive the offending person and move on without bringing it to his attention. Silent suffering does nothing to resolve the conflict, nor does it allow either participant to understand or learn from it. To handle conflict in that fashion isn't healing; it is merely the absence of pain.

It's a MUST!

In fact, as difficult as this may be, once you ascertain that you have been treated unkindly you are mandated by God to hold the other person accountable. Proverbs 27:17 describes iron sharpening iron; it is crucial to provide that sharpening (kindness) so that the relationship can be restored to its full potential. In my own experience, there's nothing quite as comforting as knowing someone loves me enough to tell me the real truth even if the process by which it is revealed is uncomfortable (Proverbs 27:6).

This Is It!

Let me guide you through the process of kindness, which will enable you to address the situation in a godly manner. As you prepare yourself to discuss the problem with the person who wronged you, ask God for the grace to be Christ-like in your attitude, words, and actions. The peace generated by that prayer will instill within you a sense of safety that will diffuse a potentially difficult interaction.

Therefore, neither one of you will require a "limo window" in order to survive the ensuing conversation.

Conflict Resolution Using Kindness

Just as the motive for patience is internal fact-finding, kindness describes what to do with what God has shown you through thought and prayer.

Step One:

Go to the other person (let's call him Fred) and ask in a non-demanding manner if he is ready to discuss the problem further. If Fred is willing to talk, then proceed according to the guidelines listed below. If not, respect the need for more time. Resist the temptation to push for immediate resolution; this will create unnecessary friction as Fred will feel coerced and manipulated. You must choose to step back (patience) for the time being, even if you think you are being deliberately shut down. Bide your time and check back later to proceed.

DO NOT USE DELAY AS AN EXCUSE TO AVOID THE CONFRONTATION!!

God will know, my friend, and so will you.

Step Two:

When you are both ready to discuss the issue, use the process of facts, feelings, and personal insights. For example:

"When you said _____ I felt _____
and I'm not sure you meant it that way."

This mirrors the LSMU process used in your patience prayers.

I urge you to use your own terminology as you move forward in this step. There's no faster way to rile Fred up than to suddenly turn "preachy" or "psychological" on him! Use your normal tone of voice and way of speaking; just make sure you get this same idea across. Otherwise, Fred will become defensive and you will get frustrated.

Step Three

If God has revealed a wrong attitude on your part, it is important that you apologize for it before going any further. Show that you are willing to take responsibility for your own mistakes. It will demonstrate that you are offering safety while still being spiritually useful.

Be specific—none of this "I'm sorry if I said anything wrong" nonsense. More like "Fred, I'm sorry I attached an electronic shocker to the remote control so that every time you turn it to the hunting channel you get buzzed." Ask Fred to forgive you for your wrong behavior (even if he refuses to admit his own wrong behavior in this situation). Be careful not to apologize only so you can get an apology in return. That would be manipulation, plain and simple.

So only say you're sorry if it's true.

Step Four:

Here is where many attempts at reconciliation go terribly wrong. We get overzealous and lose sight of what we're trying to accomplish if we try to address more than one issue at a time. This is especially true if the discussion is going surprisingly well. We get careless and accelerate as we start bringing up something that happened last week or the week before that had nothing to do with this confrontation. Then the hackles rise and a new fight erupts.

DO NOT DISCUSS OTHER PROBLEMS OR RELATED ISSUES!

State that you only want to understand his mind-set;

you could be wrong, you don't have to be right. **Make it safe for him to be human like you are.**

Let Fred have imperfections that may need to be addressed through repentance and change, just like you will need grace on issues you will struggle with in the future.

I often laugh at my tendency to want to be right all the time. Most of us in a relationship feel the same way; we focus on one flaw our mate has and continue pecking and pecking until the person either gives in or gives up. It is vital that we keep in mind our own dealings before God before we rush to change someone else (Matthew 7:3–5).

Step Five:

Ask Fred about his/her thoughts and feelings (facts, feelings, personal and spiritual insights). At first you will probably get a negative response, especially if prior interactions were less than positive. *Be patient* (submit) and listen closely even if you don't agree with his or her assessment.

You are investing in future communications with Pat; remember that your current behavior will influence his or her willingness to be vulnerable next time. If you sense that you are becoming defensive or angry, ask God to enable you to be strong and hang in there.

Let's Be Really Real Here

The reality of Agape love requires self-control and continued submission to the Holy Spirit's power working in your mind, will, and emotions. You will have to make a choice to submit to God in maintaining a normal relationship with Pat while the problem is being resolved. No cold shoulders, disappearing acts, or slamming doors, please.

In fact, it is imperative that you maintain an approachable attitude in all aspects of LSMU. Just as we are able to interpret the thoughts and attitudes of those dear to us, they can decipher ours. Also, I'm sure you have endured a difficult interaction only to feel that you've been "tuned out." You sense that you are being seen but not heard. This is a defense mechanism that allows Fred to *look* connected, while he is actually hiding in an effort to be protected from the onslaught of difficult emotions.

In a conflict, the goal is to be peaceful and spiritually useful to the point where this defense mechanism is unnecessary. Even the confrontation is to be executed in a manner that allows differences of opinion without total destruction.

Conflict is usually seen as a power struggle; if you're right then I must be wrong. If that is true, we are risking everything we value if we lose. However, if the motive behind spiritual usefulness is merely to clear the air and share insights, the risk is significantly lowered. Each success in conflict will engender a confidence that the process of kindness does work.

I have to choose to be kind on a daily basis. It is difficult for each one of us; none of us has it mastered. If there is a sin nature involved, there is a lack of kindness.

Don and I learned this concept while I was in Christian counseling, but at first I was convinced it didn't work (I was the exception because I was never wrong!).

But I had to submit to God in this area. Now I find it's crucial to be truthful immediately and not blindly attack my husband in order to defend my territory. In fact, I've recently observed how ingrained it has become in our daily conversation. Don uses the phrase, "I don't have to be right" in nearly every statement from discussing his opinion on politics to his favorite television show! That demonstrates a peace that only develops through safety and an understanding of God's involvement in this process.

Kindness to Yourself

We are our harshest critics. There is often a double standard that makes it permissible for someone else to have flaws but not us. If this reminds you of the concept of rudeness, you're one discerning reader.

Many of the concepts of I Corinthians 13:4–8a are interwoven as they all deal with our behavior and attitudes. The origin of anger is thought/opinion/judgment, which leads to the attitude of impatience. This is revealed as rudeness and lack of kindness. Our intention is to stop the cycle of broken thinking; only then can we move forward into Christ-like thoughts and attitudes toward ourselves and learn to rely on our Heavenly Father for help through our daily challenges.

Shake it Off!

Yet another perspective on personal kindness is our tendency to excuse our misbehavior and play the victim. It's the "oh well" attitude which infers that we're stuck being inappropriate and everyone else will just have to adjust. "That's just the way I am" is a good clue to a lack of kindness to yourself and others.

It's like seeing a dirty towel on the floor and ignoring it. Step over the towel often enough and you don't see it anymore; it becomes a part of your home décor! But for our family and friends it appears deliberate and selfish.

Our persistent weaknesses get to be that way. Take interrupting as an example. Many of us get so involved in a conversation we might cut someone off in mid-sentence so we can share our view. Soon it turns into a habit that pervades every interaction we share with someone else. We are so used to it we are unaware that it is hurtful and disrespectful. Eventually, this behavior stunts our relationships as we find ourselves isolated and wonder what happened. If we are able to be kind, or spiritually useful to ourselves, we can identify the cause and take steps to overcome it.

It isn't being harsh or critical, nor is the motive to condemn or punish. Rather, it is the willingness to care enough about who you are as a child of God to be able to accept reality.

Remember how I stated earlier how militant I have gotten about kindness? Having been the recipient of a lack of kindness, I am a strong proponent of knowing what the problem is so I can go before God and sort it out. The same is true about personal kindness in terms of owning up to my own quirks and tics. To be able to approach the Lord in humility with an apparent issue and learn the truth is freeing. To know I'm not stuck being inappropriate because I'm a flawed individual engenders a sense of gratitude to the Holy Spirit. The hope I experience allows me the strength to persevere through the process of change.

I hope you never lose your desire to grow and change. Improvement is a good thing, but we need to recognize areas that need work in the first place. I find it amusing that we pray for understanding of God's will in our lives, and when He reveals areas that need further work we assume it's a failing!

Show Me Where It Hurts...

As I counsel hurting people, my primary goal is to unearth broken areas in their lives. To do this we must fully discuss past mistakes and habitual sins. I'm sure it gets frustrating since often folks just want short-term answers to long-term issues.

But that's not my purpose. I want to teach clients how to repair broken parts with God's help. Not just for today's specific problems, but for every situation that will arise for the rest of their lives.

Biblical kindness is important because it gives us the impetus to rely on God's ability to speak to our hearts and objectivity to accept admonition. Moreover, it affirms the relationship He promises His children.

Spiritual usefulness ultimately allows us to exhibit respect to ourselves and each other. It creates a sense of peace that assures that there is no hidden agenda or secret sin.

It enables our friends and loved ones to recognize that the rules have not changed in the middle of the game. They have value as we speak the truth to them in love and commit to being spiritually useful in all situations.

As you learn to recognize kindness, it will be easier to accept it from individuals who have your best interests at heart. Even better, situations that were once considered random trials in our lives will now be interpreted as God teaching us more about our potential and His spiritual usefulness.

NINE

Don't Forgive Too Soon!

All along I have stressed the need for honesty and genuineness before God. We do get angry and react inappropriately. Those of us who truly desire to be godly have tried many methods to regain control over our emotional responses that haven't worked.

Rudeness and lack of kindness are just two ways in which we beat ourselves (and others) up when we feel overwhelmed and hurt. But surprisingly, there is another behavior that creates anger: feeling required to forgive before we are ready.

Many good and well-meaning Christians encourage the act of forgiveness as a means to aid in spiritual growth. Yet I suggest that to forgive too soon could be a dangerous source of anger; allow me to explain my reasoning.

Forgiveness is tricky. Part of the problem with the old definition of patience and kindness is that it assumes that any anger is inappropriate. We expect that if we just work hard enough and pray long enough we will eventually quench the fire of anger. Never mind that verse after verse of Scriptures describe the anger of God; anger over injustice, ignorance, selfishness, etc. (Psalm 7:11), (Genesis 18:19), (Nahum 1:2), (Revelation 6:16). If anger is a sin then we'd have to logically assume that God is a sinner.

WRONG!

The difference is the reason for the anger. His anger is righteous while ours is more often unrighteous.

But by ignoring the LSMU process of thinking, praying, and taking personal inventory about the situation, we add one more wound to a heart that is already breaking.

We don't allow ourselves the time to acknowledge the pain experienced in the conflict. The need to grieve is neglected, as is the opportunity to process our emotional state and admit to ourselves and to God, "I don't like it! It isn't okay with me! It was wrong and I am suffering! Why won't anyone listen to me?"

When a person claims to forgive a transgression immediately after the offense, the right to think about it further and the time to pray it through is surrendered. The belief is that since God forgives and forgets, the wronged individual must follow suit. When the inevitable touchiness and anger surfaces along with recurring bitterness, this person feels stuck in emotional quicksand that is inescapable.

This particular attitude about forgiveness has caused the hurt individual to be victimized twice: once by the transgression itself, and again by the pressure to forgive immediately. There is no allowance to FEEL hurt. What an injustice in the name of mindless obedience!

For example, if a husband is unfaithful to his marriage vows but then confesses and asks for forgiveness, the wife feels required to not only excuse the sin (because he asked, that's why), but then is not allowed to ever think about it again. So when the pain and confusion flows over her as she processes the incident later, she also experiences guilt at her seeming inability to move on. As if it's *her* fault there is a problem. Then when (not if) she finds it difficult to act as if nothing had ever happened between her and her husband, he is likely to accuse, "And you call yourself a Christian; a real Christian is supposed to forgive."

I can't tell you how many broken hearts pass the threshold of my counseling office. And most of these individuals rationalize the wrong behavior of someone else, insisting that it has been forgiven.

Oh, really?

Then why the presence of depression, anxiety, anger, guilt, and loss of spiritual progress?

When the painful layers are peeled away, most folks admit that they are still wounded, angry, hurt, and disillusioned about the situation they've supposedly forgiven. The act of forgiveness was perceived as a necessary part of healing and yet no healing was taking place. Why? Because the wife was not allowed her time to rant and rave and apply patience to the situation.

It would be akin to a huge splinter being lodged in your eye, and instead of removing the splinter first and cleaning the wound, a bandage was applied over the wound, splinter and all. That makes no sense.

No, the splinter must be removed, the wound disinfected and bandaged so it may mend properly. Then time must be allotted to ensure adequate healing; that's why doctors always recommend their patients go easy on themselves while this process occurs. Would you go jogging on a broken leg?

But Christians don't allow themselves downtime for healing. They assume that it is ungodly to sit back and take stock of their feelings, spiritual or otherwise. They often quote Scripture verses about God being their strength, yet ignore the fact that His strength implies that we can be weak.

So let's be practical at this point. What should be done when someone confesses to having wronged you and asks for forgiveness? What is an appropriate response when you sense you are being pressured to give an answer right then in the situation?

Remember that you have the right to use patience here. You must take time to stop, think, and pray before you can give an answer that is both meaningful and permanent.

Now is *not* that time.

So your attitude must be one of cooperation but firmness:

"I am sorry for this situation; I care about you. I need to spend time thinking and praying about it. I'll let you know when God gives me an answer."

Under no circumstances is it okay for you to forgive when you can't even think straight! To do so is to surrender your emotional responses in the future regarding these circumstances. So you *must* reserve your forgiveness until you can offer it freely.

Yes, we are to forgive. Absolutely and irrevocably. But not before we go before God, dig through the rubble of the painful incident and discuss it thoroughly with our heavenly Father.

I'm not suggesting you obsess over it because that would be unhealthy. No good would come of you swallowing all that rat poison. But I compare it to being a burn victim; the burnt tissue must be removed to allow fresh, new skin to form. It is painful and difficult to endure, but necessary for healing. When we forgive too soon we might as well deny the injury, all the while choking on the smell of burnt flesh. Gross analogy, I know. However, it is pretty accurate if we were to describe the pain many Christians experience, all in the name of forgiving and forgetting.

Rudeness is to continue pretending that you sailed through the crisis and are so saintly they're carving a shrine in your image. But to be kind to yourself (spiritually useful) is to admit that you have been hurt, defrauded, taken advantage of, and you don't like it.

Eventually you will forgive, because you will come to a point in your spiritual life that you must forgive in order to proceed further. But when that happens, it will be for your own health and spiritual well-being and not because you felt required to do it. You make the decision and choose to forgive; it is not to be wrenched from you like a mugger grabbing your purse. It is a gift to be given despite the pain it requires to be that generous.

Spiritual stubbornness is a good thing. The word "stubborn" has such a negative connotation. To be stubborn is to be mulish and unmovable—obstinate, headstrong, uncompromising. Perseverance is another term for it (I Cor. 13:7).

Spiritual stubbornness reflects INU2Y thinking described in Chapter Two. When you forgive is no one else's business; it's an agreement made between you and God. That means that *only you* can determine when the right time is for you to take that step. What is most important is that you do ultimately choose to forgive when the time is right.

So there.

Forgetting

To forgive and forget is a contradiction; to forgive is to acknowledge a wrong and overlook it. To forget implies that the transgression has been erased from our memories.

One acknowledges that something occurred and the other implies that it didn't! Huh?

This concept has been the cause of many wounded spirits. As believers we hear the phrase "forgive and forget," but it is often quoted too easily.

If it is so important to forget, why does Scripture emphasize the importance of remembering? In the Old Testament, each time something meaningful transpired the individual was instructed to erect an altar to acknowledge it (I Samuel 7:12), (Isaiah 19:19,20), (Joshua 24:26,27). God stressed the need to remember the sins of our fathers, the faithfulness of our God. If God says we need to remember, why do we think we need to forget?

We must remember in order to bookmark our experiences. We are to acknowledge the situation and the lessons we retained from it—good and bad. We learn from both good and difficult lessons. If I burn my hand on a hot stove, I remember that painful sensation next time to avoid committing the same blunder.

Physical and emotional scars are monuments to successes and failures in our lives; the brave things we've done and the not-so-smart stumbles we've endured.

So when we refer to forgetting, the idea is to be able to remove the pain of the situation, all the while using the knowledge gained from the experience itself. To forget is to emotionally heal from the effect the transgression had in your heart and life.

I have several scars on my hands and arms, all due to thoughtless acts in my youth (and also in my not-so-youthful days). Each scar represents a situation where I was injured in some capacity, whether accidentally self-inflicted or otherwise. As I catch sight of them I am reminded of the pain I suffered during the experience.

Like everyone else, I also have emotional scars incurred

from unhealthy interactions in my past. While regrettable, these scars cause me to recall the lessons I learned from having lived through them. Am I to ignore the bells, whistles, and sirens I might hear if I find myself close to being hurt again?

No.

We are never to forget the lessons learned from these scars. Nor are we to be blind and clueless when similar situations arise and we find ourselves in the same predicament.

For example, imagine you have a teenager who has been doing poorly in school. The school administrator has called and reported that John has been skipping classes and was caught smoking pot at a friend's house.

John is truly repentant and promises profusely that he will never do anything like that again; it was a one-time deal. So you forgive. But several weeks go by, and you begin to notice that John still isn't bringing home any schoolbooks, nor is he showing any improvement in his class attendance. Plus he's acting dopier than usual.

Do you keep your suspicions to yourself because you've forgiven John in the past and forgiveness implies forgetting?

No.

You use the past experience with John as a reference point by which you are reminded of his behavior in the past. You don't get overly emotional about it; you simply stop, think, and pray for wisdom about the situation and take appropriate steps.

There is a difference. In the past, forgetting has been perceived as a final step in forgiveness, but if that is so we lose the benefit of forgiveness.

When I accepted Christ into my heart and life, I did so with joy and gratitude at the forgiveness freely offered me. I continue to remember who and what I might have become had that forgiveness not been accepted. I feel it would be presumptuous to forget what was sacrificed so I could have the gift of eternal life.

God promised in Jeremiah 31:34 that our sin He will remember no more. This verse is often cited as evidence that we should be that forgiving. I want you to notice that it takes a holy God to have the ability to do that! When He declares that we are forgiven, He means that the former sin in our hearts is erased. God has not erased the memory of the sin, but rather the deserved punishment of that sin.

The longer I experience the grace of God, the more I appreciate the difference between what I thought I knew about Him and what I have learned since studying the concepts of LSMU. Not because this is an idea I grasped onto as a client of Christian counseling; rather, because I have seen it work time after time in the lives of hurting people. How completely He provided a means by which we can take responsibility for our personal relationships! Yet when we make mistakes, He loves us in spite of our "falling shorts."

When I see the "ah hah!" expression on someone's face who finally understands that it doesn't matter what other people say or think or do, it just blesses me so much. To understand that God wants each of us to claim the rights we have as His children, bratty or angelic, is incredible.

What it all boils down to is that we can accept not only the salvation He offers, but also the daily relationship we can have to become more of who He created us to be. It's called confidence in Christ. The confidence in the relationship between you and your heavenly Father ensures a godly partnership (of course, He owns more shares!). Once you experience the success of being able to hear God and gain the ability to be spiritually stubborn, you'll grow in that confidence.

I know this is true because of who God is.

TEN

If God Is God

I remember vividly the cozy office where I met with my Christian counselor, Dr. Dan Wilkinson, for the first time. Stuck in my brain during my "I'm-scared-and-broken-and-nobody-can-fix-me-not-even-God" days was a hand-stitched picture on his office wall. Created by a grateful client, it was beautifully rendered in mellow shades of orange and brown. Written on it were the words, "If God Is God…"

Those words intrigued me, first of all because I had never heard that phrase before despite my lengthy association with Christianity. Next, I was puzzled because I felt unsettled by the open-ended statement; it was as if I could fill in the blanks myself at any time regarding any situation.

After I had been meeting with Dr. Dan for quite some time, I realized that "if God is God" was a standard statement of his. As Dan taught me from Scripture who God is and who I am as His child, Dan would say, "Well, if God is God, He'll do what He promises," or "if God is God, He has the power to hear your requests," or "if God is God and His Word is true, then He can't lie..." and so on.

Those four simple words have stuck with me even after all my years of training and counseling other individuals as wounded as I had been. If God is God and He makes a promise, He can't fail. He won't fail. If God is God and He says He loves us with an everlasting love (Jeremiah 31:3), then that's all we need. If God is God and He claims He loves us as His chosen children, then He means it.

So in our times of anger and unkindness and rudeness and hasty forgiveness, if God is God, He loves us anyway! We don't have to pretend or feel oppressed by our perceived frailties. If God is God, He'll accept us because He created us.

It Doesn't Come Naturally

I grew up in a home where none of us really understood the meaning of unconditional love. It isn't that we wouldn't have offered it to each other, or withheld it from each other. We simply wouldn't have recognized it if it stood in front of us under a neon sign barking like a dog.

It wasn't until I became a mom that I got an inkling of what love really felt like.

I finally understood that a parent can love her child and not like the child's behavior. But that child is still fiercely and completely loved.

I'm sure most of us can remember a time when one of our kids did something so out of whack we could only shake our heads in amazement (that's when they take after their dad...). We can also recall incidents when the offense was punishable, but the kid looked so cute we could hardly keep a straight face! Case in point is the unsupervised make-up lesson or the works of art on the freshly painted walls. My own dad claims I was a terror with a crayon as a little tyke, but it's his word against mine…

Who among us parents hasn't shuddered when being informed that little Suzy told her entire kindergarten class that her daddy made her mommy cry this morning?

I strongly believe that God experiences the same emotions we do; sometimes we really mess up, lose our tempers, and say something hurtful or embarrassing. After the dust settles, we are sitting on the ash heap of remorse as we reflect on our actions and the punishment we're certain we deserve. I'm not saying God overlooks our sin; at times we do need to be chastised, just as our own children need correction. In spite of that fact we never stop loving our children, and, if God is God, He'll never stop loving us either.

So if God doesn't condemn us for our failings, what gives us the right to condemn ourselves? My sense is that deep down we suspect that God let us off easy. He promises to forgive, but we determine we need to suffer more than that. Therefore, despite its availability, we don't accept His forgiveness.

Think back to my early belief that I only got into heaven due to a loophole in Scripture: "Whosoever will…and Karen…may come." While it seemed natural to claim that I was unworthy of His grace, the more I learn of Him (and myself through kindness) I wonder if I was really asserting that God wasn't really God. Or at least He wasn't the God I thought He should be. After all, He forgave my many sins simply because I asked Him to! How could He love me that much? I ruefully confess that I expected Him to behave like the angry gods depicted in those cheesy jungle movies I used to watch as a kid. You know, the ones that had the terrified maidens getting pushed into fire pits while natives pounded on drums fashioned from animal skins. Overdramatic picture perhaps, but true.

Less Imagination, More Truth

But the God of Scripture isn't that capricious. In fact, from what I read He's forthright in His willingness to forgive (Psalm 86:5), (Matthew 6:12) (I John 1:9), (Psalm 85:2), (Matthew 9:2), (Ephesians 4:32), (Psalm 103:3).

What I really had to admit was that I was being arrogant in my opinion that if He wasn't going to do His job, then I'd have to do it for Him. I was supposed to hurt more, to suffer more, to twist and writhe in repentance until God was satisfied that I'd paid my dues.

But finally, I had to concede that if God is God, His promises are true. I can't pay for something that has already been purchased. I'm astonished at the requests I've made for God to transform me into something I already was: dearly loved and completely accepted. I can't work to become what I already am: a redeemed, albeit tarnished, child of the Living God.

How cool is that?

Enough Already!

During my Bible college days I was active in the musical chorale. We traveled often, as we performed for local churches of all shapes and sizes on the weekends; one Sunday may have found us at a very large church while the next weekend the choir members often outnumbered the church attendees.

On one particular Sunday our director was informed that due to the limited seating capacity, and the fact that it was a special Sunday with many visitors, we would have to stand and wait outside the front of the church building during the service, only coming into the sanctuary to perform.

While we waited, several of us altos found a small ledge to perch on so we could rest our feet as much as possible. Being experienced performers by now, we knew to speak softly and move as little as possible so we would not distract anyone inside the church. As a small group of us gathered, we noticed that occasionally an older man would approach a few of us, say a few words, and leave. Each time this gentleman returned he appeared more agitated.

Finally, even our group was distracted when the gentleman turned and looked at us. Pointing in my direction he said, "Miss, would you please move your head away from the doorbell?"

Unbeknownst to me, I had chosen the only area in the front of the church that housed a small doorbell; each time I changed position on the ledge I pressed the button!

So while the announcements and introductions were being made, the sermon preached, and the visitors welcomed, a doorbell was pealing through the sanctuary!

As God bends His head and His heart to listen to our prayers and fellowship with us, I wonder how many times He thinks, "Hey, I've heard that one already! You already *have* that; you already *are* that. You don't have to keep pushing the same button—You're already *in*!"

Does God think we waste His time? I don't believe so. But we could be so much further in both our relationship with Him and in our confidence in His continuing love for us. I challenge you to resist the desire to push the same doorbell over and over in your quest to be victorious in your Christian walk. You already *have* victory!

Eleven

Bandages or Armor?

I have been sharing this formula of LSMU to give you tools by which you can be responsible for your actions and reactions during times of conflict. It is a choice you must make daily; when you recognize progress I want you to begin to enjoy a new sense of hope. When you look back on the pitfalls inherent to any interaction, you will be able to identify the work of the Holy Spirit in your attitudes and behaviors.

It won't happen overnight! As useful as this process is, it takes continued application to become proficient; it took practice to learn to apply make-up, so will this (and you won't need perfect eyesight or a steady hand to succeed...).

But it is vital that you allow yourself grace to fully embrace LSMU for it to become second nature. It won't come easy; if you've been flying off the handle for most of your life, it will take more than one or two attempts to excel.

However, I urge you to persevere. If you lose your cool ten times but at the end of the tenth time think, "I wonder if LSMU would have worked?" you're making progress.

We are in essence attempting to bend an iron bar (*aka* our tendency to get angry) and turning it from one fixed position to an entirely different shape. It will take time and much application.

Now is the time to engage your spiritual stubbornness. I suggest you start by focusing on your physical response to the conflict, the heat in your chest or sweaty palms, and automatically say, "Lord, Shut Me Up!" No reasons or explanations are needed; remember, you're going by faith that the Holy Spirit will reveal the problem to you.

In the meantime your goal is to learn to trust that physical reaction so you don't push yourself off the waterslide.

So learn this process, tuck it away in your heart and mind so it becomes a part of you. It will take practice and stubbornness, but it will work for you. The worst feeling in the world is realizing that a painful situation could have been avoided if you'd only used the information you already knew but ignored. Even in those conflicts when you feel wounded and overwhelmed, God will comfort and nurture you. But He'd much rather hug you in victory than soothe your self-inflicted injuries.

GOD WILL PROVIDE BANDAGES, BUT HE'D RATHER GIVE US ARMOR!

He has given us a means by which we can gear up for the battles we are destined to wage. Struggles with anger, rudeness, lack of kindness, and guilt are daily skirmishes faced by anyone who must interact in this world.

We have a choice whether we're going to run away or stay and fight the battle. We also have a choice of weapons. Emotional outbursts, hibernation, or even physical attacks are weapons that in reality harm us more than our perceived enemy ever could; the resulting remorse causes painful scars that take years to overcome.

However, the patience and kindness described in this material arm us with peace and reliance on God. Frankly, I'd much rather hide behind my Heavenly Father in conflict rather than strike out using my own puny strength. After all, who can fight God and win?

No More Mrs. Nice Guy

So, my friends, isn't it assuring to know that God doesn't expect us to like sipping tea? He never set up the standard to look right and act right, but feel all wrong— *we did.*

In our feeble attempts to be pleasing, we lost sight of who we really are: genuine, fabulous, and imperfect.

Please take this to heart. In our quest to be more like Jesus Christ, it's really not up to anyone else to decide what God's plan is for our lives. INU2Y reminds us that if we're to answer to God for our life decisions, then we'd better learn to decipher them for ourselves. Knowing that we've already received eternal life by accepting Jesus as our personal Savior, the only task left to us is that of refinement. It's ridiculous to pray for something we already have; would you continually push the doorbell to be let into a room within which you're already standing?

Let's focus on who we already are and enjoy the gifts we've been given. To criticize ourselves and others is to insult the One who carefully chose the components that make each of us unique.

You Aren't a Loophole!

May you experience the joy and encouragement that comes from successfully using the information contained in these pages. How awesome it is to know you aren't a broken, useless vessel cast off by God! Reliance on Him will aid your ability to control your anger as you learn to pray:

LORD, SHUT ME UP!

References

- Amplified Bible

- Holy Bible New International Version

- Living Love, Cognitive Biblical Therapy, Dr. Daniel Wilkinson

- The Oxford American Desk Dictionary and Thesaurus, Second Edition, Berkley Books, New York July 2001

- Strong's Exhaustive Concordance of the Bible

Lord, Shut Me Up!

Anger Management for Christians

Study Guide

Karen D. Wasoba

CONTENTS

LSMU Study Guide

ONE

Real vs. Ideal

Please allow me to carefully welcome you to the study guide for my book, Lord, Shut Me Up!

I say carefully because I'm very aware of the risk involved in such a study; I'm going to ask you to reflect upon your own life, behaviors, and their consequences as we journey through its pages together. Will it be interesting and fun? Yes and yes. Will it be challenging? I hope so. Will it make you mad?

Ummmmmmm....if so, it will give you a great opportunity to practice what you've learned from reading the book.

My hope is that you surrender your mind, will, and emotions to God as you process this information. If you feel overwhelmed or emotional, step back for a few moments and catch your breath. Then resume the work that will enable you to break through the angry walls that have held you back from experiencing the real joy promised to you.

Smile Like You Mean It!

There is a universally held belief that Christians should only exhibit positive emotions such as those listed in Galatians 5:22.

Gallatians 5:22: _____

_____

_____

_____.

But what about real life? Look at Galatians 5:22 again. What if my current circumstances:

- Causes me to not feel _____ .

- Not experience_____ .

- Not sense _____ .

- Or have enough emotional energy for_____ .

- Or I'm too busy for _____ .

- Or am too exhausted to display _____ .

- So it makes me question my _____ .

Doesn't it seem as if everyone else has a handle on stress and you don't?

Guess What!!

EVERYONE gets flustered, irritated, aggravated, hassled, and ticked off and wants to find someone to punch in the head or a hole to crawl into.

Every living, breathing being has had to deal with people, places, or things that cause disruption in the course of life. Even if the situation is unreasonable or untrue, even if it's not you but them, not this but that, the upsetting circumstance has had an effect on you, your family, and your faith.

So What's the Question?

So....how do we deal with it? Do we adapt to the situation? Or do we kick and scream and make it very clear to everyone within earshot that it's simply not okay with us?

What is your first reaction to people, places, and things that make you angry? _____.

_____.

_____.

_____.

Does it make the incident go away? _____.

Does it make you feel better? _____.

How long does the satisfaction of having lost your composure last? _____.

_____.

Do you end up making sandwiches (if you've read LSMU you know what I'm talking about)? _____

_____.

Why Am I Picking On You?

Stop a moment and think about the last time you lost your cool. What did you do afterwards to try to make amends to the other person? _____

_____

_____

_____.

Did you feel emotionally satisfied with the outcome? ___

Time to tell the truth

Share what it's like to be you; how often do you have to repent of your anger and promise God you'll never trip over your tongue again? _____

_____

_____

_____

_____

_____.

Let's go waaaayy back

Can you think of the first time your frustration caused you to lose your temper? Share what happened: _____

_____

_____

_____

_____

_____

_____.

Did that experience have any influence on your current
attitudes? _____

_____

_____

_____

_____.

What comments are often used to describe you? (I get
called 'weird' a lot- as if that's a bad thing…): _____

_____

_____

_____

_____.

Do you feel as if you're defined and/or limited by your
temper or identity as an angry person? _____.

Does that definition truly describe who you are? _____.

How about spiritually? Do you cower before God after
you finish venting?_____

_____

What do you think God expects from Christians as far as self-control?_____

_____

_____

_____.

Whoa now.

Before you beat yourself up about what you think you should have done, stop here and catch your breath. In… out…..in….out.

Better?

Okay now. Let's review what we read in Chapter One of LSMU.

Real vs. Ideal

Good Christians don't get angry. They cheerfully believe that any and all frustrating experiences in their lives are spiritual tests and thus pass them all easily. Their apparent serenity is in direct opposition to what the 'rest of us' face daily.

Proverbs 15:1: _____

_____

_____.

Proverbs15:18:_____

_____.

Proverbs 16:32: _____

_____

Proverbs 21:9: _____

_____

_____.

Proverbs 21:19: _____

_____

_____.

Proverbs 22:24, 25: _____

_____

_____.

Proverbs 25:24: _____

_____

_____.

Proverbs 25:28: _____

_____

_____

_____.

Proverbs 29:9: _____

_____

_____.

Proverbs 15:18: _____

_____

Psalm 37:8, 9: _____

_____

_____

_____.

Ecclesiastes 5:2:_____

_____

_____.

Colossians 3:8:_____

_____

_____.

Summarize what these verses say about anger: _____

_____

_____

_____

Did you know there were that many verses about anger?

_____.

The verses seemed to echo the idea that our anger can damage the quality of our lives, our relationships, and our self concepts.

As you think of the overall theme of these verses, share your personal insights: _____

_____

_____

_____

Humbling, isn't it?

Not so Fast!

Now before you get all cocky because you don't yell, scream, or throw things when you get mad remember that it's the *heart attitude* that's important. Do you hibernate and shut down when you get aggravated? Is it difficult for you to open up about what is troubling you? Do you give folks the cold shoulder when they approach you or even worse, mislead them by saying "Nothing" when they ask you what's wrong?

GOTCHA!!

Anger can run hot or cold but ultimately it's still anger. While following this study guide you must examine your thoughts and feelings. Be honest about what's going on inside your heart.

Share what you thought the last time you became angry:

_____

_____

_____

_____

_____

How did you actually behave?_____

_____

_____

_____

_____.

I bet you even congratulated yourself with the thought, "At least I didn't _____

_____

_____."

I <u>knew</u> it!

Do you think you got away with it? _____.

I shared in LSMU that I always felt like a pretender in church and an afterthought in the eyes of God due to my emotional turmoil. I was convinced that a good Christian never reacted the way I always did to stressors.

Revelation 22:17:_____

_____

_____

_____

_____.

Do you see any loopholes in there?

What Do We Do Now?

The biggest hurdle Christians face is not that we deliberately rebel before God. We would gladly follow the Lord in doing what He wants us to do if He would only tell us EXACTLY what it is.

The problem is we _____ _____ what we_____ _____.

We often don't have enough information about a situation; then indecision creates a lack of confidence to act appropriately. When we ask for advice from our Christian friends, no two opinions are alike.

Then no matter which action we choose we are left with the consequences while our 'advisors' go on merrily with their own lives.

Have you ever felt that way?

What we need is a plan

Lord, Shut Me Up! is based on I Corinthians 13:4-8a.

Love (God) is_____.

Love (God) is _____.

It does not _____.

It does not _____.

It is not _____.

It is not _____.

It is not _____.

It is slow to _____.

It keeps not a _____ of wrongs

Love does not delight in _____ but with the _____.

Love _____.

Love (God) always _____.

Love (_____) always _____.

(He)_____.

Love (God) _____.

—*I Corinthians 13:4-8a*

Are You In or Are you Out?

The goal of this study guide is to teach you what you may not know. There will be hazards ahead as you face thoughts and behaviors from the past that have not worked. First of all, you need to take personal responsibility for your own contribution to conflict. Own up to your bad attitudes and resentments; God knows about them anyway, my friend!

I Chronicles 28:9a: _____

_____

_____

_____

_____.

Hebrews 4:12: _____

_____

_____

_____.

Two

Patience

Many Christians get their definition of patience from Sunday School class and church sermons (and Mom on Christmas morning…). There are Biblical commentaries solely on that topic as well as a multitude of secular and non-secular books on the subject.

For our purposes we want to distill it to one short sentence. Here are a few ideas:

Patience is…..

- Endurance in suffering,

- Bearing up under pressure without complaint,

- To wait unflinchingly,

- Tolerating inappropriate behavior aimed at us personally,

- Accepting leftovers while everyone else gets the best choices.

Do you have any other ideas?

Patience is: _____

_____

_____

_____.

Who is the classic example of patience in the Bible?

_____.

How do you compare your own burdens to what this person experienced? _____

_____

_____

_____

_____

_____.

Patience implies that we are to sit, wait, and do nothing while we allow ourselves to be taken advantage of and accept such treatment without complaint.

Agree_____.

Disagree_____.

That seems to be a pretty long sentence after all, doesn't it? I think we can be more concise.

Patience means we do nothing and think nothing while other people and situations run over us.

Not short enough?

Patience = they win/we lose.

Shorter?

Patience = victimization

Stop here for a moment and think. Has that thought ever occurred to you? Yes or No

If no, that's great. You may go get an iced drink. But come back.

Now for the rest of us.

That thought has occurred to me. Often. I've chafed under the impression that dying to self and accepting unfair treatment just didn't seem right.

My dictionary's definition of Patience is:

> 'n. calm endurance of hardship, provocation, pain, delay, etc.' (p. 1093)

Synonyms of patience: tolerance, forbearance, restraint, toleration, stoicism, fortitude, endurance, sufferance, submission, resignation.

Sounds....awesome.

When is the last time you requested prayers for patience at a meeting of fellow Christians? What was their typical response? _____

_____

_____

_____

_____.

I've noticed that some folks even flinch a little at that request.

They think that to request patience is to invite misery and punishment in order to learn to deal with it. So asking for it seems just plain nuts.

The genuine meaning of patience is to wait upon God for the truth before acting. It is the act of sticking with a situation to learn all the facts. Patience is to hang in there until the situation is fully revealed, and to demonstrate self-control in the meantime.

Interpret the above meaning of patience in your own words: _____

_____

_____

_____

_____

_____.

Is patience supposed to be active or passive? _____.

Why? _____

_____

_____.

I'm Conflicted!

Our attitude about conflict will determine how we utilize patience. Most believers are convinced that any disagreements are unspiritual and that any relational discomfort is wrong.

Because of that attitude, most conflict is seen as an accident waiting to happen. No good can come of it so it is best to just avoid it.

If I Close My Eyes, Maybe You'll Go Away

Do you know someone who will avoid conflict at all costs? _____.

Does this behavior encourage peace or does it make it worse? _____.

From LSMU, what is the name for the tendency to go to sleep mentally, emotionally, or spiritually?

_____.

Hibernation is a survival technique that creates no new conflict and makes no waves. It is static in that it does nothing to change the situation. It may work well for bears but hibernation serves no purpose but to lose time.

There is no learning or growing with hibernation; anyone in conflict with these folks grows even more aggressive when they observe no satisfactory reaction.

Describe a time when a conflict accelerated in order to obtain a reaction, whether positive or negative: _____

_____

_____

_____

_____

_____

_____.

How do you think the aggressor might have perceived the situation? _____

_____

_____

_____

_____.

Was hibernation the best choice? _____

_____

_____

_____.

If A Little is Good, a Lot More is a Lot Better

The other main reaction to conflict is <u>overreaction</u>. Act first, think later.

Overreaction is defined as the tendency to 'make too much of a thing, make a mountain out of a molehill, lose all or one's sense of proportion, go too far.'

> (p. 1066)
> 'Better to be silent and be thought a fool than to speak and remove all doubt.'

Ecclesiastes 5:2: _____

_____

_____

_____

_____.

Proverbs 29:20: _____

_____

_____

_____

_____.

James 1:19: _____

_____

_____

_____

_____.

Proverbs 19:1: _____

_____

_____

_____.

Those of us with short fuses overreact frequently. We summon up old memories, grudges, and experiences to interpret current events and jump haphazardly into the middle of the situation in an effort to fix it all. We think we see the conflict accurately and enter talking. We claim we are only being truthful. It's not our fault if someone takes offense at our actions.

Who do you think of in the Bible when we discuss rashness or overreaction? _____.

Who do you think of currently?_____.

Wwwwhat Happened?

People who overreact are often as surprised by their behavior as anyone else. The triggering event is usually so minor that the resulting explosion catches everyone off guard.

I Really Blew It

Several years ago our family experienced some serious financial trouble. For many months Don was unemployed while the expenses piled up. Finally one of our old cars broke down. Then another car broke down. Through it all I was amazed at my serenity. Despite being a chronic overreactor, I was surprisingly calm throughout the situation. Smugly, I convinced myself I had become proficient at coping with trials.

One day during all these troubles, I decided to treat myself to a piece of candy from a gum machine we kept in our kitchen. In my zeal to get a particular piece, I shook the machine and accidentally shattered the globe. Bubble gum and glass scattered all over the kitchen floor.

I was inconsolable for two days!

What's the Number for 9-1-1?

It wasn't the gumball fiasco that pushed me past my boiling point; it was just the final event that made my emotional strength crumble.

In your daily life, what are the little irritations that you encounter? _____

_____

_____

_____

_____

_____

_____

_____.

Do you tolerate them until you blow up and lose your temper? _____.

Does that solve the problem? _____.

Both _____ and _____ serve to create a sense of unease among those of us who encounter them on a regular basis. Either reaction to conflict prevents us prevents us from being objective and seeking the truth in the situation.

Because we are uncomfortable and frustrated we flare up over even unimportant incidents. We react to the often normal behaviors of others, and find ourselves watching their tics and twitches rather than being honest and responsible for ourselves.

Read Matthew 7:3-5 and summarize:

_____

_____

_____

_____ .

Also Luke 6:41,42: _____

_____

_____

_____

_____.

Who, ME?

It's much easier to blame someone else for causing us to be jerks than it is to just admit we were wrong. Read Genesis 3. Adam and Eve had trouble accepting responsibility from 'The Beginning...'

Let me stop you there, Buckaroo

Before you jump on our ancestors, let me remind you of something important. While Adam and Eve had a perfect relationship with God, they didn't have any experience at all with blame, finger pointing, and acknowledging sin. They didn't even know what sin was (but hey, they *started* it...).

You have had a lifetime to live, observe, have successes and failures. Many prayers have been spoken and requests made to God. We are responsible for ourselves, our ongoing relationship with God and those whom God has placed in our lives.

Admit it!

You'll notice that one recurring theme in LSMU is personal responsibility.

I'll bet that means I want you to take _____ _____ for all of your thoughts and actions.

Take _____ _____ for your attitudes and need for honesty.

Take _____ _____for what you will learn in this study guide.

THREE

Anger

Where Anger Begins

Not everyone has the distinction of having the nickname "Temper Tantrum."

The majority of adults have learned how to control themselves when faced with maddening circumstances. Externally, that is.

However, internally is where the buzz of activity occurs. Our perception of the problem begins the downward spiral. Our eyes or ears capture the activity. Then the data swirls around in our brains, our brains come up with a conclusion, and we act accordingly.

There is a lot at stake if our initial perception of the problem is based on incomplete information. Friendships have ended miserably due to a lack of information. Promising careers never got off the ground, relationships have died, and entire families have been devastated by misunderstanding.

No Sense, No Feelings

Wouldn't we all be better Christians if we had no senses?

No sense of sight—Can't see someone's behavior.

No sense of smell—Can't complain if the litter box wasn't emptied. Continue with your own examples:

No sense of taste: _____.

No sense of touch: _____.

No sense of hearing: _____.

Thinking is Risky

The first step toward anger is a *thought*. I notice that my husband left the cupboard doors open (again). The more I think about it my memory kicks in: I've asked him to close those doors many times and he still leaves them open.

Step One: _____.

The next step toward anger is the *opinion*. We can think about or observe something without becoming angry.

But when we form an opinion about it the issue becomes important.

My husband left the cupboard doors open:

It must be an evil plot.

He's doing it on purpose.

He doesn't care that it matters to me.

Step Two: _____.

The most dangerous step toward anger is *judgment*. Our opinion about who did what to who leads us to determine that our rights have been violated and whoever caused that crime must pay.

Step Three:_____.

Note: Anyone who has ever tripped over an inanimate object, then picked it up and thrown it forcefully understands how pointless anger can be sometimes. The object (Toy? Shoe? Book?) was there before you were and yet it's an evil monster that must be destroyed. We feel sheepish about it later, but at the time it engendered a major rage.

List the steps to anger:

_____

_____

_____.

Then it's WAR!!

Describe your behaviors once you've reached the judgment stage: _____

_____

_____

_____

_____.

Are you able to stop yourself? _____.

Stop and think about the last time you really lost your composure (Whether you caused it or not).

Recall the thoughts you had that bounced around inside your brain.

Do these words sound familiar?

- "That's not fair"

- "I should..."

- "I have a right"

- "Just wait until..."

Do you stay mad?_____.

What's the longest amount of time you've been angry/hurt to the point you couldn't move on?_____.

Referring to LSMU, have you ever "eaten rat poison?" If so, describe the experience: _____

_____

_____

_____

_____

_____

_____.

Was it worth it?

Did the earth stop spinning, people stop in their tracks, conversation cease? Did birds stop singing, babies quit crying?

I didn't think so.

But it's all about ME!

Is it?

Before you slam this workbook shut in exasperation, let me explain myself.

When we are in conflict, it is so easy to lose perspective. We think only of our feelings and the person/situation that smashed them flat. Only after we've bandaged our own wounds do we go to God and ask for "His Will" to be done. I don't know about you, but at that time "His Will" should be replaced with "my will" since I know what needs to be done.

We pray that the *other person* change, be taught, be corrected. Not that WE learn, change, and grow through it.

What do you do when the spotlight of responsibility shines on you? _____

_____

_____

_____

_____

_____ .

Excuses are useless in the presence of God.

Have you ever tried to excuse your attitudes and behaviors in your prayers to God?_____.

Were you able to divert the blame to someone else? _____.

When you communicate with your Heavenly Father, He

loves you and wants you to be real before Him. Remember—He knows your thoughts!

A vital component of anger management is the ability to accept your own bad attitudes, exhaustion, biases, and judgments that contribute to the conflict.

Read and summarize Psalm 51:1-4:_____

_____

_____

_____

_____

_____

_____

_____.

Let me add this…

This is not to say ALL conflict is your responsibility so just sit there and clam up about it .

NO!

But before we can learn what TO do for anger management, we must learn what NOT to do… and that is to make it everyone else's fault.

In the Beginning...

Anger that begins as a _____, becomes an _____, then dissolves into _____.

All anger is our decision; sometimes the decision is made for us if the situation is obviously against what is taught in Scripture. We must not contradict_____.

But the other cases are up to_____.

Four

Pride

The commonly accepted definition of pride is of an overbearing opinion of one's worth or importance (p. 1183). When we describe someone who is proud we think of egotism, conceit, and arrogance.

Believers work hard on humility; in fact, they're proud when they achieve it.

Pride is independent thinking apart from God and/or the unwillingness to be submissive to God before reacting to a situation.

Pride is _____ _____ apart from God.

Pride is the unwillingness to be submissive to God _____ _____ to a situation.

Let me clarify, however: pride is often motivated by fear. We often experience fear in the midst of a conflict; then our _____ triggers the 'I have to win this argument no matter what' instinct to survive the conflict.

Often pride appears when a person feels inferior, hurt, angry, mistreated, and misunderstood. The result is prideful behavior.

- Pride is when I act rebellious toward God, am unwilling to listen to God; when I refuse to stop hurtful attitudes, words and actions toward myself and other people.

- Prideful behavior is when I desire to be in control (or I'm too frightened to NOT be in control).

- Pride is when I pick and pick at someone to win the argument despite my heart knowing I'm hurting them or the relationship.

- Pride is being unwilling to listen to other opinions (I might be threatened emotionally).

- Pride is when I claim that I am 'good enough,' 'better than YOU.'

- Pride is when I expect my friends and loved ones to accept the statement, 'That's just the way I am' to justify my thoughts, attitudes, and actions.

- Pride is when I want what I want when I want it regardless of the consequences.

Does this definition of pride surprise you? _____.

Briefly describe your impression of these examples of pride: _____

_____

_____

_____

_____

_____.

Have you ever heard anyone make the comments listed?

_____.

How would hearing those comments make you feel?

_____

_____

_____.

List two statements you've heard that are examples of pride:

1. _____.

2. _____.

Have you ever made any of these comments yourself?

_____.

Is it safe to state that some conflicts are based in pride and that sometimes people are just too scared to be calm in a conflict? _____.

Could pride make us wade into a conflict without thinking about it because we automatically defend ourselves?

_____.

I've reacted blindly to conflict so many times it's embarrassing. My fear and insecurity convinced me that everyone and everything was a threat. I believed that there must have been a secret society somewhere that held regular meetings focusing on how to reveal my flaws to humanity. Therefore, I was poised to meet my foes head on, even anticipating a threat when no danger existed.

It was a nightmare.

No One Else To Blame

I finally had to admit that I was being prideful in my attitude. Really, it wasn't all about ME after all.

There were no 12-step meetings being held in my honor; in fact, most folks probably hadn't given me, my comments, or my appearance a second thought.

I didn't need to win as I related to other people, I just had to relate.

Here's God's View

We are still responsible for our behavior even if its origin is based on insecurity. God has plenty to say about pride:

Psalm 101:5:_____

_____

_____

_____.

Proverbs 8:12,13:_____

_____

_____

Proverbs 13:10: _____

_____.

Proverbs 16:18: _____

_____

_____

_____

_____.

Proverbs 18:13: _____

_____

_____

_____.

Proverbs 28:25: _____

_____

_____

_____.

Ecclesiastes 7:8,9: _____

_____

_____

_____.

I Timothy 6:4: _____

_____

_____

_____.

I Timothy 6:17: _____

_____

_____.

James 4:6b:_____

_____

_____

_____

I John 2:16:_____

_____

_____

_____.

Man, the Bible is pretty serious about the subject of pride!

Pride must be addressed personally and privately between you and God.

Yes, it MUST be addressed if you're the prideful one. But when in conflict you mustn't use your opponents' pride as a point of debate. It will only confirm their fears and make them fight harder and use meaner weapons.

Has this chapter on pride been a surprise to you? If so, what concepts are new to you? _____

_____

_____

_____

_____

_____ .

FIVE

Rudeness

You are probably wondering why we haven't even hinted at *how* to control our anger. That's because we need to sort out *why* we get angry in the first place. Trust me in this process- we'll get there.

Rudeness can be defined as being impolite or offensive. When a person is being rude there is an absence of respect and protection. Rudeness is exposing someone's weaknesses and mocking them, then acting as if you didn't know what you were doing.

Often described as 'feigned ignorance', I like to call rudeness what it truly is:

Playing stupid.

I know you've experienced this phenomenon: you've been caught saying something mean or being a jerk. All eyes are on you just waiting for your response.

So you deny it. With your eyes wide open and your fingers crossed behind your back you deny you've done anything wrong.

Rudeness is when your verbal arrow hits its mark and makes the intended target flinch in pain. Instead of apologizing you accuse your victim of being overly sensitive.

What is rudeness often known as? List both.

1. _____ _____.

2. _____ _____.

Rudeness hides itself. It is the subtle disrespect paid for an unwelcome comment or behavior. Rudeness is disguised as humor; we make critical comments and observations about ourselves and others. Then if we offend someone we hide behind the joke.

Matthew 10:25: _____

_____

_____

_____ .

Rudeness is evident when we turn the blame on others to avoid personal responsibility.

"I'm only kidding."

"Can't you take a joke?"

"Lighten up."

Raise your hand if you've heard any of these comments.

(I'm counting, I'm counting...okay, you can put your hand down now).

Raise your hand if you've ever made these comments yourself.

(Wait! I can't count that high!)

There is always a motive behind rude comments. Sometimes the motive is to be sarcastic. Sometimes we want to let it be known that all is not as it appears.

Rudeness can be demonstrated by body language. What particular gestures or actions seem rude to you? _____

_____

_____

_____.

Have you ever been wounded or angered by someone's nonverbal behavior? If so, what did you see? _____

_____

_____

_____

_____ .

Angry facial expressions are obvious signs of rudeness. But there are many subtle expressions of rudeness such as muttering, eye rolling, foot stomping, sighing, and closed body language. Whatever method is used, disapproval is being communicated without uttering a word.

Proverbs 10:18: _____

_____.

_____.

Proverbs 20:14: _____

_____

_____

_____.

Isaiah 5:20: _____

_____

_____

_____

_____.

James 1:8: _____

_____

_____

_____.

These verses describe a rude person: someone who says one thing yet means something else entirely.

Rudeness depicts a hidden agenda.

Stop and think for a moment. Have there been times when you've sensed conflict or been uneasy when the reason hasn't been obvious? Have you every asked someone if something was wrong and they've denied it?

If so, share your experience: _____

_____

_____

_____

_____

_____

_____

_____.

If I Had Half a Brain...

Don't forget about the rudeness we show to ourselves, the criticism hidden behind jokes and negative comments. It is a subtle warning to others that we're flawed and to not expect much out of us.

Hebrews 10: 25:_____

_____

_____

_____

_____

Rudeness is a lack of _____.

Rudeness covers _____.

Rudeness can be aimed at _____ as well as at others.

Rudeness isn't just allowing my mind to focus on the negative aspects of life, but is also an embellishment of shortcomings and a desire to be demeaning. I am not protective, but identify and magnify your weaknesses so that you are mocked and embarrassed.

Rudeness can be expressed in very subtle ways such as body language in response to someone else. Or it can be shown in more obvious ways like verbal ridicule while in the presence of others.

Rudeness means _____   _____.

Whether you observe it coming from you or coming at you, rudeness must be addressed. Spend time this week asking God to make you aware of your tendency to be rude and for the ability to surrender that behavior to Him.

Six

Lord, Shut Me Up!

Patience has already been discussed in Chapter Two of this study guide.

Remember that patience is not *hibernation*. What is hibernation? _____

_____

_____

_____ .

It is not *overreaction*. What is overreaction? _____

_____

_____

_____ .

Patience is waiting upon God for the _____
before _____.

According to this definition, we are to wait for the truth of
the situation. Does that mean we never act upon what we
learn? _____.

Who are we to wait upon before we act on our perceptions? _____.

Why?

_____

_____

_____

_____.

White Knuckle Living

There is usually a physical reaction when conflict is immi-
nent. For some people it appears as a knot in the stomach
or they grit their teeth. Many folks clench their fists, get
nauseated, or their body temperature increases.

Think for a moment. When you sense conflict- your own
doing or someone else's- what is your physical reaction?

_____

_____

_____

_____

_____.

Have you ever considered those signals as a warning sign from the Holy Spirit? _____.

Often we interpret the symptoms as proof that we have a right to behave the way we do. Then we wonder what we did wrong.

The very presence of this physical response means there's also an emotional response to the situation. Something scary is up ahead, just around the corner. It's a potential monster coming to swallow us whole.

Stop Everything!

You've been watching too many spooky movies, my friend. In reality, we have input into what we do and say. We are not victims waiting to be slashed and burned; nor are we villains waiting to nab and gnaw on an unwary prey.

Back to our emotional and physical response: the reaction is a signal that something is amiss. The trick is to keep those feelings from controlling your thoughts and actions. Your fear is not meant to be a springboard for your escape from conflict.

What are the two types of response to conflict?

_____ and _____.

Which usually comes first? _____.

There must be automatic obedience at this point and we must practice in order to make it automatic. None of this mindless reaction that leaves everyone wondering what just hit them.

It's coming! It's in the room with me!

AAARRRGGGHHHH!!

I'm sweaty, I'm clenching, I'm irritated, I'm tired, I'm aggravated, my stomach hurts, I'm gonna lose it......

Now is the time to respect the Holy Spirit speaking to your heart and mind.

Respond by saying:

"Lord, Shut Me Up!!"

Step 1: Lord, Shut Me Up!

Remember, the prayer is NOT "Lord, shut me _____."

You aren't in any condition to make good decisions right now.

Rely on (circle one):

- *yourself
- *your spouse
- *your pet hamster
- *Holy Spirit
- *your pastor

...to help you step aside emotionally to gather facts about the situation.

Don't run away. If you do you have no facts to present to God as you seek the truth about it.

Stay there physically unless you feel threatened physically. Although many people claim that walking away helps them not say damaging things during a fight, I know walking away only makes most people even angrier.

Stop talking or arguing about the conflict. Excuse yourself mentally for the purpose of taking time to think and pray.

Explain why you should stop arguing:_____

_____

_____

_____.

Many experts recommend walking away during a conflict. I disagree. Why would it be a bad thing?_____

_____

_____

_____

_____

_____.

How do you excuse yourself emotionally? _____

_____

_____

_____

_____.

It is critical to keep in mind that this exercise has a purpose. It is so you have the _____ you need when you take time to think and pray.

Step 2:" Help Me Hear You"

Your goal is to maintain your composure during the conflict. This involves a level of submission before God and a willingness to hear so you can gather the facts intelligently.

Do you _____ during a conflict? Do you stare blankly at the situation, using _____ _____ to stay there but don't actually hear what is going on?

Seeking grace from God will give you the ability to submit your _____, _____, and _____ to Him in this situation.

IN THIS SITUATION!!

Don't freak out at the first sight of disagreement. Remember that the initial conflict is of short duration.

What makes the problem seem to last for days or even weeks:_____

_____

_____

_____ .

Proverbs 14:29: _____

_____

_____

_____

_____.

Psalm 18:2:_____

_____

_____

Step 1 of LSMU: "_____

_____."

Step 2 of LSMU: "_____

_____."

Imagine you are a medical doctor attempting to diagnose a seriously ill patient. Do you look at the patient's chart, recall the last meeting you had with them, and walk into the appointment with a set diagnosis?

If so, you won't be in that career for long.

No, you collect data, take samples, consult with colleagues, and research the textbooks for more information. It is necessary for you to have as much information as possible so you can treat the person effectively. Once you have determined the illness you begin a course of treatment to enable the patient to regain his health.

The same is true for anger management. It would be impossible to successfully process the learned information if you haven't learned the information!

Step 3: "Here are my facts…"

State the literal facts to God AS YOU SEE THEM concerning only this _____. No extra opinions or editorials. No referring to yesterday or last week.

Step 4: "Here are my feelings…"

Be specific. Present your findings based on your experience. Say it all, don't hold back anything that's going on in your heart and mind.

Romans 8:26: _____

_____

_____

_____

_____.

THIS is the time to have the temper tantrum! Go on- express yourself in any way you want. God can handle it and besides, He knew you had it in you. He knows you, your heart, and your pain, and loves you anyway.

Step 4 is not for God's benefit. It's for _____.

Get it off your chest. Vent and complain and make sure you say everything you want to say.

Stick only to the current _____.

Step 5: "Am I right?"

Ask God to show you if you've been truly wronged in

_____   _____ .

Are your feelings justified? Did you walk into an ambush due to someone else's actions? Seek to calmly hear Him as you spend time in _____ and acknowledge your feelings about this conflict.

Step 6: "Am I wrong?"

Was I having a lousy day? Was I too tired, hungry, vulnerable, sick, or flustered? Was my own fuse remarkably short?

As you keep your heart turned toward the Holy Spirit weigh your own possible contribution to the conflict.

Once we are rested and fed and prayed up, the Holy Spirit often reveals that we started it in the first place. (I hate it when that happens).

But if it does happen, the best part of using LSMU and keeping the attitude and behavior under wraps is that there's no one you have to repent to but _____. You won't have to make amends with anyone else and you definitely won't have to make _____.

No other apologies are necessary.

NOT SO FAST!!

This process will take several days in the beginning. It is a new _____ and it won't come naturally. (Self-control rarely comes naturally).

Psalm 25:5:_____

_____

_____

_____ .

While you wait for God to reveal the _____ to you, submission/obedience to God means you will not:

Show rudeness:_____.

Example of rudeness:_____

_____

_____.

You will not:

Show pride: _____ apart from God.

Example of pride:_____

_____.

You will not:

Show anger: T_____, O_____, and J_____.

Example of anger: _____

_____.

And you may not lie, because these actions, however justified in your thinking, are not _____ -like.

IT'S YOUR RESPONSIBILITY!

Should you discover that your attitudes and behaviors in this situation are to blame for the latest conflict, confess them as _____. Ask God (the Holy Spirit) to convict you of _____ _____ and _____.

Take care of it. Then move on in your life.

Remember: You cannot control another person's behavior, but you can control your _____ to that behavior.

SEVEN

Kindness

The Biblical definition of kindness is to show oneself to be spiritually useful to yourself and others.

Ephesians 4:32: _____

_____

_____.

Christians seem to portray kindness as being (ugh) *nice*. Jot down some words you'd often use to describe nice (and you can't use 'kind'):

_____

_____

_____

_____

Look back at your list. Do the words describe strength or weakness? _____.

Remember, we live how we perceive ourselves to be.

So if believers feel they must be:

- Mild

- Sweet

- Unassuming

- Meek

- Quiet

....they might set themselves up to be weaker than God ever intended.

Read Joshua 1:6,7, and 9. What phrase is repeated in these verses?

_____

_____.

Ephesians 4:15a: Speak the truth _____

_____.

It does not say to be 'nice.' It says to be truthful. But there is also a warning as it specifies 'in love.'

We are cautioned that when we are spiritually useful to another person our motivation must be love for them and their potential. If not, we are not being kind, we might just be … nice.

When attempting to speak the truth in love (kindness) the most important thing to consider is your _____.

_____.

Galatians 6:10:_____

_____

_____.

Proverbs 27:6: _____

_____

_____.

Proverbs 27:17: _____

_____

_____.

These behaviors do not describe kindness:

- Not telling someone that their behavior is hurting themselves or someone else. It is unkind to know how to help a person grow emotionally and spiritually and not do anything about it.

- Being fearful that telling the truth will cost you a friendship.

- Not sharing your true feelings when you are asked directly.

- Trying to be a peacemaker no matter what.

Share your own experiences with kindness (positive or negative):

_____

_____

_____

_____

_____.

One question to ask yourself regarding kindness: "Would I want someone to tell ME?"

If the answer is 'yes' then you must love them enough to speak the truth _____ _____.

It is hypocritical to expect other people to treat you differently than you are willing to treat them.

Kindness = Confrontation

It is vitally important that you go through the process of LSMU for the truth of the situation. Give yourself time to sort it out. This will result in your ability to be calm and reasonable as you continue with the process of patience.

Next, kindness comes into play. Whether the problem originated with you or someone else, you are still _____ to reconcile the matter.

As difficult as this may be, once you determine that you have been treated poorly, you are mandated by God to be kind, or _____ _____.

Eight

How to Demonstrate Kindess in Conflict

Conflict Resolution Using Kindness

<u>First</u>: Go to the other person and suggest you discuss the issue. If they are not ready, respect their need for more time and tell them you'll check later.

You don't want to push for a resolution. Why?_____

_____

_____

_____

_____.

Have you ever been pushed to talk about something serious before you were ready? _____.

How did it end up? _____

_____

_____

_____.

Delay can be an excuse to avoid the confrontation completely. Don't do it!

<u>Second</u>: When you are both ready to discuss the issue, it is important that you _____ if God has revealed a wrong attitude or behavior on your part. Be specific and ask for _____ for your own wrong behavior.

Why should you acknowledge your own responsibility early in the confrontation? _____.

_____

_____

_____

_____.

Matthew 7:3: _____

_____

_____.

Luke 6:41:_____

_____

_____.

<u>Third</u>: State that you only want to understand what really happened: you could be wrong; you don't have to _____ _____.

Make it safe for them to be human like you are!

We often perceive conflict as a power struggle; if you're right then I must be _____.

But if the motive for _____ is to merely clear the air and share insights the risk is significantly lower.

<u>Fourth:</u> After you share your facts, feelings, and spiritual insights ask him about his thoughts and feelings.

Listen closely and be calm even if it hurts or you don't agree.

God will enable you to be _____ and persevere.

NOTE: In a conflict, the goal is to be peaceful and spiritually_____ to the point where _____ or overreaction is unnecessary. Even the confrontation can allow differences of opinion without total destruction.

Kindness ultimately allows us to respect ourselves and each other. It creates a sense of peace that assures that there is no hidden agenda or secret sin.

Now it's your turn. What have you learned about the concept of kindness? _____

_____

_____

_____

_____

_____

_____ .

Let me challenge you: In your interactions this week, seek to identify (in yourself and others) those who use kindness and those who are simply nice.

Journal it here: _____

_____

_____

_____

_____

_____

_____

_____

_____

_____

_____

_____

_____

_____ .

After all that, name someone who demonstrates kindness

_____.

Would you go to _____ if you need the ab-
solute truth?_____.

Pray that God would make you spiritually useful in someone's life today.

NINE

Don't Forgive Too Soon!

Forgiveness is to Christians as global warming is to environmentalists. It's an emotional subject and everyone has an opinion about it.

Name four attitudes that can contribute to anger:

1. Lack of _____ not seeking the truth from God.

2. Lack of _____ or spiritual usefulness.

3. _____ or feigned ignorance.

4. _____ or independent thinking before God.

Each of these issues, if not recognized and dealt with, can greatly inhibit spiritual and emotional growth. Relationships suffer, and conflict escalates.

But there is yet another issue that causes Christians to

question their very belief system if not addressed properly. That issue is forgiveness.

Many dear, well meaning believers stress the importance of forgiveness. It is the cornerstone to spiritual health.

Matthew 6:14: _____

_____

_____

_____.

Luke 6:37:_____

_____

_____.

Ephesians 4:32: _____

_____

_____

_____.

Do you believe in forgiveness?_____.

Is there anyone who you can't or won't forgive?_____.

Forgiveness is essential. Full joy, peace and growth can not be experienced without the willingness to forgive.

The ability to forgive doesn't come naturally. When we are injured and bleeding emotionally the last thing we want to do is let the offender go unpunished.

Remember our discussion regarding fairness? If someone

hurts us or someone we love it just is not fair to let them get away with it,

Right?

Ultimately, we realize that the only way to achieve peace of mind is to surrender our hurts and grudges to the care of our Heavenly Father. Through this action we are relieved of the burden of keeping score.

Yet, a great disservice is done to victims when the attention is taken away from the offender. It is then placed on the offended with the expectation that they are required to forgive the hurt.

Have you ever had that happen to you?_____.

A trauma can be recent and the attitude of our Christian brothers and sisters is to forgive and move on. So not only do we have the traumatic event to deal with, but also the responsibility to forget about it.

Now THAT'S unfair.

No wonder we limp around in a state of numbness. Confusion reigns.

The pressure to do what other people think you should do in this situation is crushing.

Share your experience with needing to forgive:

_____

_____

_____

_____.

Did you feel pressured to forgive too soon? _____.

How much spiritual and emotional damage might it have done to you? _____

_____

_____

_____

_____ .

Are you amazed by people who seem to find it easy to forgive horrendous acts taken against them? _____.

I think of parents of murdered children who claim to forgive the killer. I'm reminded of wronged spouses and slandered ministers.

I have to be honest with you—I don't think I would be that accepting of the wrong done to me.

> I'd kick
> And scream
> And yell
> And cry
> And then I'd do it all again.

Because I want to be genuine before God despite what the opinion of other people might be.

Because if I forgive too soon I'll be limiting my ongoing need to vent, think, pray, and cry before God.

Think of the psalms of David. Here are just a few verses:

Psalm 3:1-4; Psalm 5:1,2; Psalm 6; Psalm 9:13; Psalm 22.

David had plenty to think about. He needed to forgive and

to be forgiven. David freely vented, and ultimately was able to surrender his feelings to God.

The definition of Patience: Waiting upon God _____ the _____ before acting.

Step One for anger management: _____

_____!

The prayer is not 'Lord, Shut me down.' To forgive we must be able to take the time to hear God speak to us about the situation.

This is between you and God alone.

No one else's input or opinion.

Before you can perform the action of forgiveness you must wholly submit your mind, will, and emotions to Him

_____

_____.

Step Two: "Help me _____ You"

You must maintain your composure in the face of trials. You're spending your time NOW as you deal with the pain rather than having to admit later on that you just weren't ready the first time.

No one can go through the process but you.

Sometimes it seems as if well-meaning folks push us to forgive quickly in order to make themselves feel better. Then they continue on with their own lives, leaving us alone with our bleeding hearts in our hands wondering what happened.

Kindness to ourselves means we can't let that happen!

We must "speak the _____ in love" to ourselves at this point (Ephesians 4:15a). We need to admit that we are in no condition to make any decisions at this point.

Not that we are unwilling.

We just can't.

As a counselor, I often hear clients speak of death and dying, transition, and trauma. It is understood that change takes time.

No one expects a hurting person to be able to make serious decisions when they are so emotionally wounded.

Not so with forgiveness. It's as if the victim is supposed to have a push button that if pressed will remove the pain.

So to be kind, or _____ _____, we must take the time we need to process the information and wait for God's leading. No matter how much pressure we experience to do otherwise, or how much we love and respect the person urging us to forgive for our own sake.

And then what?

Eventually, the pain of being angry will weigh more than the pain of forgiveness. The healing process will demand that we begin the rehabilitation of our hearts and minds. But only then can we forgive.

Forget THIS?

I Samuel 7:12 describes how an altar was built to commemorate a time when God was with Samuel.

To forget merely refers to the pain involved in the trauma, not the trauma itself. It means to surrender the grudge.

You must take the time to forgive. Then it's final.

TEN

If God Is God

Titus 1:2:_____

_____

_____

_____.

Hebrews 6:18: _____

_____

_____

_____.

What do these verses say about God?_____

_____

_____.

God cannot lie. In all of His vastness, there is not one bit of lie or deception in Him.

Cool, huh?

Jeremiah 31:3: _____

_____

_____

_____.

Romans 8:16,17: _____

_____

_____

_____.

I John 4:10: _____

_____

_____

_____.

John 10:27, 28: _____

_____

_____

_____.

God calls us His _____.

Matthew 7:9: _____

_____

Since God cannot lie, then all His statements are true. He says we are His children and that He loves us with an everlasting love.

If God is God He means what He says.

Can we say that about ourselves?

Have you ever made a promise and couldn't keep it?

_____.

Have you ever disappointed someone who trusted in you? _____.

Has anyone ever let you down when you depended on them? _____.

But that's DIFFERENT...

It's ironic that we will believe what we think about ourselves but won't believe what God says about us. If Uncle Ned claims we'll 'Never amount to much, no one in your family ever did" we'll believe it and let it keep us defeated.

If God says we are fearfully and wonderfully made we want a thirty page thesis and references from an ivy league school before we'll consider it.

Psalm 139:14:_____

_____

_____.

That's backwards if you ask me.

If Uncle Neddy and God has a difference of opinion, who wins? _____.

If your best friend and God have a difference of opinion, who's right?_____.

If your Mom and God don't agree, who's right? _____.

If you and God are in conflict, who's going to win? _____.

Because I Said So!

If God is God (and He is!) then it only makes sense to take His Word for it.

He is our Parent, and He can steer us in any direction He desires.

Matthew 7:7-11: _____

_____

_____

_____

_____

_____ .

Luke 20:36: _____

_____

_____

_____ .

Galatians 3:26:_____

_____

_____.

If God is God He keeps His promises. What He says is true. Share what that means to you: _____

_____

_____

_____

_____

_____.

ELEVEN

Bandages or Armor?

Throughout this entire study the focus has been on your
_____ before God.

Lord, Shut Me Up! is based on the verses: _____

_____

_____.

Love is _____.

Love is _____.

It does not _____.

It does not _____.

It is not _____.

It is not _____.

It is not _____.

It is not _____.

It keeps no _____.

It does not _____

But _____.

It always_____.

It always_____.

It always_____.

Love _____.

Love _____.

The goal of this study guide has been to teach you what you may not _____.

Just as we must teach our children how to grow to be responsible adults, so God teaches us to be responsible in our spiritual growth. It would be unreasonable to expect us to automatically know how to deal with everything the world throws at us; so God wants to give us armor to be prepared for the daily challenge of living for Him.

Romans 13:12: _____

_____

_____

_____ .

Read Ephesians 6:11-18.

It tells us to put on the whole _____ of God, and then lists in detail the different portions of armor:

Stand therefore, having your:

Vs. 14: Loins girt about with _____,

And having on the _____

Vs 15: and your feet shod with the _____

_____

_____.

Vs16: And above all, taking the _____

_____

_____.

Vs. 17: take the _____

_____

_____,

And the sword of the _____, which is the

_____.

Now after reading those verses, does it sound to you like God doesn't care about you? _____.

Do you think that He wants you to be prepared for battle? _____.

The battle is not always with an obvious enemy. Sometimes the battle is with: _____.

Lack of _____ or not seeking the truth from God.

Sometimes it's our misguided attempts to be 'nice' to other people, even if we know they're doing or saying the wrong thing.

Often we avoid telling ourselves the _____ about our own attitudes and behaviors.

When we are not spiritually useful to ourselves and others, we are not being _____.

Rudeness means _____ _____.
It's a way of displaying anger without being obvious; it can be sneaky, mean, and insulting.

Have you considered how often you are rude to yourself?

_____.

When you have put on the armor of God you are safe from the wounds of anger, pride, and rudeness. Conflict doesn't have the same frightening effect on your heart and mind when you know you can not lose the battle.

So It's a Sure Thing

Yes, God is our Healer. When we are deeply injured it only makes sense to let the Great Physician tend to us.

Psalm 103:2,3 says: _____

_____

_____

_____.

It doesn't say 'might' or 'could.' It states that He heals ALL our diseases. God has whatever bandages you need.

He's got the biggest doctor's kit in all creation!

But the coolest thing is that He wants us to avoid the pain that unresolved conflict and anger can cause in the first place. These steps to anger management, known as Lord, Shut Me Up! will guide and encourage in the midst of battle:

Step One: "＿＿＿＿＿＿＿＿＿＿＿＿＿＿＿＿！"

Step Two: "＿＿＿＿＿＿＿＿＿＿＿＿＿＿＿＿."

Step Three: "＿＿＿＿＿＿＿＿＿＿＿＿＿＿＿."

Step Four: "＿＿＿＿＿＿＿＿＿＿＿＿＿＿＿."

Step Five: "＿＿＿＿＿＿＿＿＿＿＿＿＿＿？"

Step Six: "＿＿＿＿＿＿＿＿＿＿＿＿＿＿？"

Conflict doesn't last forever (it just feels like it). As you practice these steps you will discover that disagreements don't always guarantee failure.

Your attitude and response will change; therefore, the degree of conflict will also change.

Before too long you'll realize that you haven't blown your fuse for a while.

Maybe for quite a while.

Maybe pets and family members won't flinch when you make a sudden move...

Use the process of Lord, Shut Me up! and with God's help, you can succeed in the area of anger management.